BUILDING CLASSIC ANTIQUE
FURNITURE *with* PINE

BUILDING CLASSIC ANTIQUE FURNITURE *with* PINE

BLAIR HOWARD

BETTERWAY BOOKS

CINCINNATI, OHIO

METRIC CONVERSION CHART

TO CONVERT	TO	MULTIPLY BY
Inches	Centimeters	2.54
Centimeters	Inches	0.4

Building Classic Antique Furniture With Pine. Copyright © 1998 by Blair Howard. Manufactured in China. All rights reserved. No part of this book may be reproduced in any form or by any electronic or mechanical means including information storage and retrieval systems without permission in writing from the publisher, except by a reviewer, who may quote brief passages in a review. Published by Popular Woodworking Books, an imprint of F&W Publications, Inc., 1507 Dana Avenue, Cincinnati, Ohio 45207. (800) 289-0963. First edition.

Other fine Popular Woodworking Books are available from your local bookstore or direct from the publisher.

02 01 00 99 98   5 4 3 2 1

Library of Congress Cataloging-in-Publication Data

Howard, Blair.
    Building classic antique furniture with pine / by Blair Howard.—1st ed.
        p.   cm.
    Includes index.
    ISBN 1-55870-473-6 (pb : alk. paper)
    1. Furniture making—Handbooks, manuals, etc. 2. Furniture, Pine—Handbooks, manuals, etc. 3. Fine woodworking. I. Title.
TT195.H675   1998
684.1'04—dc21   98-4124
                                                                CIP

Edited by R. Adam Blake
Content edited by Bruce Stoker
Production edited by Bob Beckstead
Interior designed by Brian Roeth
Cover designed by Clare Finney
Illustrations by James Stuard

Jo, this one is for you.

Acknowledgments

To embark upon a project such as this one is to quickly find that it's not a one-man job. True, as far as the woodworking and writing were concerned, I did all of the work myself. But a book, especially a woodworking book, is the product of teamwork; the projects and writing are the easy parts. Beyond that, a great many people lent their efforts and talents to produce the work you are now holding in your hand, and it's to those people I wish to extend my heartfelt thanks.

First, I wish to thank Adam Blake, my editor at Popular Woodworking Books. Without his support and expertise, this book would never have seen the light of day. Adam's assistant editor, Bruce Stoker, must also take a great deal of the credit. Jim Stuard is responsible for the working drawings, some of the best I've ever seen—thank you Jim. To all of the support staff at Popular Woodworking Books and F&W Publications, thank you.

Beyond the editorial staff at Popular Woodworking Books, some other people lent a hand, gave advice and generally supported the project. To them I also say thank you, especially to the people at Delta International Machinery, Porter-Cable, Leigh Industries, American Clamping and the folks at Elmer's Glue.

Finally, and by no means last, I'd like to thank my wife, Jo. She, too, supported me throughout this seemingly never-ending project with never a complaint. This, I suspect, is because she knew she would end up owning many of the pieces that were the result of the work.

About the Author

Blair Howard's interest in woodworking began more than forty years ago in high school in England. His interest in furniture, especially antique furniture, goes back even farther. Apart from a short stint as a carpenter for a construction company, his woodworking was never more than a some-time hobby. Then, as a result of corporate downsizing, he suddenly found himself looking for work. So, the hobby became a source of income. Today, his work is much in demand and sells to all sorts of markets: galleries, furniture stores, factory outlets and to individuals. He lives in Cleveland, Tennessee.

Table of Contents

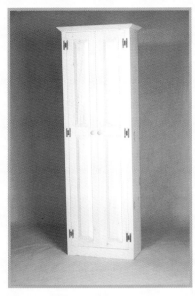

Introduction

Antique furniture has always been a passion of mine. Long before I became seriously involved in woodworking I spent many hours and days in London's Victoria and Albert Museum, and in a hundred or more stately homes in England. And I grew up amongst old furniture. Some of it was undoubtedly junk, but some was prime. I remember my mother and grandmother going to an auction sale at Wood Norton Hall, just outside Worcester in England. The hall, the one-time home of Henri-Eugene-Philippe-Louis d'Orleans, duc d'Aumale, the fourth son of Louis-Philippe, the last king of France, had just been vacated by the last of the Bourbons in exile. The two ladies came home bringing all sorts of fine bits and pieces with them, and more on the way in a van, including a pale green carpet embroidered with a golden fleur-de-lis. No, the stuff back then, around 1955 I think, didn't cost the fortune it would today, but that's another story. Anyway, my interest in all things old goes back even before then. I have dim memories of wanting to own, perhaps even to build, a paneled blanket chest in the Elizabethan style. It would be long time, however, before I would be in a position to build, let alone own, any of the wonderful pieces I thought I knew so well; and, even with the advent of this book, the Elizabethan chest remains no more than a dream.

I fell into woodworking almost by accident. True, I had taken several years of woodwork shop in high school, but it wasn't until I lost a well-paying job, due to downsizing, that I became seriously involved. An old friend of mine had a small commercial shop, and he kindly took me in and taught me the ropes and many of the techniques I still use. Today, I make my living primarily as a writer but also by making and selling reproduction antique furniture, mostly to local shops and stores and, though rarely, to order, which brings me to the next point.

The word reproduction is a subjective one; it means different things to different people. To the unscrupulous it really means "fake," and big bucks, but that's not what this book is about. To me the word reproduction means "look-alike," and, while I like to make my pieces look as authentic as possible, no attempt is made to reproduce the style, techniques, tool marks, etc., of the old masters. These are fun pieces, conversation pieces; some might even become family heirlooms you can proudly display in any room of the house or, better yet, sell for a tidy profit if you wish.

When this book was conceived I wanted it to be something special, to offer a range of projects to suit woodworkers of every level of experience. Therefore, the pieces you'll find throughout the following pages are varied from the fairly simple to the quite complex. You'll be able to use every tool in the shop, and then some. All of the projects are, I think, exceptional examples of early American furniture from the eighteenth and nineteenth centuries. They are all favorites of mine. I have chosen them not simply as a means to fill the pages, but as projects you'll enjoy building and owning. Most of them were built for the first time as I wrote the book. I had the rare privilege of filling these pages with pieces I wanted to build; many of them, much to the delight of my dear wife, Jo, ended up in our own home, replacements for mass-produced pieces bought at local furniture houses. Some are fairly easy to build; some quite challenging; all make for interesting and enjoyable hours in the shop.

Chapter 1

Materials and Techniques

The wood used for most of the projects in this book is new white pine, which in many cases is what would have been used back in olden times. Some of these pieces, however, would certainly have been made from hardwoods of one sort or another. No matter, pine is well suited to all of these projects. It's also very inexpensive, readily available at the local hardware store or builder's supply house, easy to work, forgiving and can easily be finished, just as was done by the masters all those years ago, to present the look and feel of something infinitely more expensive.

As to tools, you should know that I'm a great believer in power tools. Not for me are the handsaw, mallet and chisel of the purist, although I can understand the pride and joy that must come from doing things the old-fashioned way. However, I also believe that, had power tools been available all those years ago, Messrs. Hepplewhite, Sheraton and Chippendale would have owned and used the full range. Would their work have suffered because of it? Of course not. A master is a master no matter what the tool in his or her hands.

NUMBER 3 PINE/ SHELVING BOARD

Shelving board? Sounds kinda nasty, doesn't it? Well believe me, it's not. Over the last few years I have consumed many thousands of board feet of this delightful medium, all at less than a buck per foot, most of it at around $.80, some for much less. It comes usually in 16- or 14-foot lengths, machined ¾″ thick and 11¼″ wide. Often it's very clean white pine with few knots and checks; sometimes it's not quite so nice. You have to pick through it, taking only the best boards. Yes, most places will let you do that if you explain you're making furniture. There are some disadvantages, of course. Often this stuff is stored outdoors with only the loading dock roof for cover. This means the moisture content is often something of a mystery but always much more than is ideal, and therefore it can be quite unstable. The answer, if you have time and money to spare, is to buy a little each week and store it in a dry place in your shop for six weeks or so. Even so, you're going to find some cupping and bending, and it may be you'll have to split the boards, reverse the end grains and glue them back together again. A little extra work, but more than compensated for by the low cost of the stock.

GRADED PINE

If you own a planer, and have a lumberyard nearby, this is, perhaps, the best source of readily available pine stock. Number 1, 2 and 3 common stock can be purchased usually in widths from 6″ to 12″ and from 1″ to 2½″ thick. Often it's dressed only on one edge and one face, the other edge and face remaining rough sawn, thus the need for a planer. The moisture content is usually around 16 to 19 percent—not quite low enough, but, other than some light cupping and bending, I've experienced few problems because of it. Costs, because you're buying from the source, run lower than for shelving board, typically $.60 to $.70 per board foot for 4/4 stock, and more than enough to compensate for the extra work involved. I use a lot of this stock.

Furniture-Grade Pine

This is the best new pine stock you can buy. It usually comes rough sawn in various lengths from 8 to 12 feet, and in various thicknesses from 4/4 on up, and in widths from 4″ to as much as 14″ or even 15″. Obviously, you'll need to own a planer, which means a lot more, often heavy, work. You can have the stock dressed at the yard, but that means extra cost, usually about $.08 per board foot. Still, the stock is almost always clean, with few knots and checks, and the moisture content should be

Making a Board

 The pine used for many of the projects is readily available at any builder's yard, comes as nominal 1 × 12 in 12-foot to 16-foot lengths and is very inexpensive. It's known in the trade as shelving board, but don't let that put you off, it's good stuff; I have sold hundreds of pieces ranging in size from small wall cabinets to huge entertainment centers. If it's knotty, so much the better; this gives it character. Usually, shelving board is classed as grade three lumber but, if you're lucky, you'll find long sections clean and free of knots and checks.

Sometimes this inexpensive pine shelving board is likely to be cupped, twisted, bent or all three. It also tends to shrink, sometimes quite significantly, across the grain. This need not be a problem, so long as the warpage is not too bad. If you can, it's a good idea to buy your stock a few weeks before you need it and set it aside to dry out a little and do some shrinking. If your shop is warm and dry, this won't take long; a week to ten days at most. At the end of that time you'll find your nominal 11¼″ width is now down to 11⅛″, or even 11″, and that's good . . . .

To make your board, first rip your stock to 5½″ and then, using your jointer, true up one face, then mill one edge to 90°. Then, using your planer, true up the other face. Next, set the 90° edge against the rip fence on your table saw and true up the other edge. Now it's a simple task to biscuit and edge-glue any number of boards to any given width.

between 9 and 10 percent. It is supposed to be cut from old-growth forest, which means the grain structure is much closer with less tendency for the stock to cup and warp. I have yet to find that to be the case. Furniture-grade pine, if you take it undressed and as is, can be quite inexpensive—I've bought it for as little as $.65 a board foot—but it's not all that easy to find. Is it worth the extra work and time involved? In some instances, yes; in most cases, barely.

Antique/Salvaged Pine

This is, perhaps, the best stock of all. Salvaged from demolition sites, large-scale renovations and so on, this timber is always well seasoned, has a patina that often extends deep into the board and can be found in widths and thicknesses unavailable today. The disadvantages? There are a few. Again, you'll need a planer, lots of time and, unless you can find a contractor willing to give it away just to get rid of it, a lot more money. You'll also need to be extra careful of hidden nails and other metal bits and pieces hidden beneath the surface. These can and will play havoc with your power tools. A metal detector of some sort is ideal for searching them out; be sure to get every little piece. Many larger cities have salvage yards where you can buy this sort of stock, but from that source it's going to be very expensive and this book is about saving money. Always be on the lookout for building or demolition projects in downtown areas. Don't be afraid to stop the car and go to look. Ask for the contractor or his foreman, and ask what's available on site. If there's nothing there, ask if they know where you might find what you're looking for; the answers will often surprise you. Old pine floorboards can often be found ranging up to 2″ thick and 12″ to 14″ wide—beautiful stuff. And sometimes they'll let you have it for a song. Unfortunately, because of programs such as *The New Yankee Workshop* on public television, the word is getting out. Contractors, and in many cases their helpers, have suddenly found that what once was scrap only fit for the fire is now a new source of income, and prices for salvaged lumber are rising accordingly.

Pine By Any Other Name

Many builder's yards carry all sorts of odds and ends from the pine family: fir, spruce and the like. Often it looks a lot nicer than the shelving board, and it is. It's also a lot more expensive.

Spruce, for instance, is softer than white pine, quite fibrous and doesn't sand quite so nicely. You'll need sharp tools to work it, but the grain is straight, it takes stain fairly well and its creamy white color presents a very clean and attractive appearance. Be prepared to pay upwards of $2 a board foot.

Chapter 2

Construction

I have tried to keep things as simple as possible. Simple construction techniques are particularly important with pine, which is quite unstable and has a tendency to swell or shrink quickly.

DRAWERS

In many cases the old-world methods are the best. The lap joint is the easiest and also the original method used in drawer construction. Cabinetmakers of old avoided using dovetails when working pine because pine tends to breathe more than the hardwoods. Many of the projects in this book have drawers built using the lap-joint method. Some, however, especially the larger and more exotic pieces, do have drawers made using dovetail joints. Drawer bottoms 200 years ago were made of thin pieces of stock edge-glued together, not the plywood we use today. If you want to go to those lengths, feel free to do so.

CARCASSES

You'll find all the traditional construction methods have been used somewhere in this book, but the tendency is to keep things as simple as possible without destroying structural integrity or original lines. The biscuit jointer is a great boon to woodworkers like me, and I use it extensively but not exclusively. Where I have detailed biscuits, you can substitute dowels if you like. And nothing can replace the mortise-and-tenon construction for table legs, aprons and the like. Where dowels were once used to secure joints I use screws topped out with plugs for an authentic look, but in some cases I have used dowels too. I use nails only where nothing else will work, but I don't like to; holding power is minimal and the holes, even when filled and covered, look awful.

Frame-and-Panel Carcasses

This was the method of choice for cabinetmakers of old. Not only did it save vast quantities of expensive hardwoods, it provided room for large areas of stock to move

and breath, thus alleviating the tendency to warp and crack, a necessary consideration when working with pine. You'll find frame-and-panel construction is used for some of the projects in this book. A well-built panel is functional, aesthetically pleasing, fun to make and provides a real sense of achievement. Except where raised-panel doors are concerned, the panel will almost always be made from lauan ¼" plywood. It's inexpensive and can be sanded and finished quite nicely.

FITTINGS

To preserve the overall authentic look you should try to use the right fittings. The illustration will provide you with an idea of dates and styles. All are available, made by several companies in the United States. Ball and Ball of Exton, Pennsylvania, offers a good range; Wood-

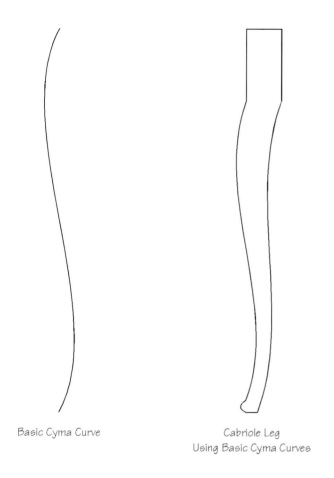

Basic Cyma Curve

Cabriole Leg
Using Basic Cyma Curves

worker's Supply and Woodworker's Store both offer limited ranges and, of course, some of the major supply houses—Home Depot and the like—offer useful ranges too. Another good source is old furniture that can often be bought for a song at auction sales.

WHAT'S IT WORTH

For the sake of fun and curiosity I've included a paragraph in each chapter that will give you an idea, and it's only an idea, of what each piece is worth in today's market. Having said that, you should realize prices will vary from one part of the country to another. What a piece might sell for in the Deep South will inevitably be less than what the same piece would sell for in New York or Ohio, for instance. I sell almost all of my work directly to the trade, to retail stores or wholesalers. Therefore, I give you both prices: trade and retail. What you get for yours depends on many factors, not the least of which is having the nerve to ask a high price and then stick to your guns when you get objections. Remember, most of the pieces described in this book can only be bought from craftsmen and women such as yourself. Factories do not make reproductions such as these. Therefore, what you are offering is something different, something unique, handmade and a point of interest not available elsewhere. You should charge for your work accordingly.

Chapter 3

Finishing

A piece of furniture is only as good as its appearance. A poorly made but well-finished piece can look, and sell, ten times better than a well-made piece with a poor finish. As location is the key to the real estate business, so finish, finish, finish is just as important in the furniture business. It takes me longer to finish a piece than it does to build it, and so it should. To many people, finishing is a chore. To me it's fun, and the final result provides me with a real sense of achievement. My best advice is take your time, think each step through and never try a new technique without practicing it several times before applying it to a piece of furniture.

How you finish the projects in this book is largely up to you. You may not want to use the techniques I've described, preferring instead a more contemporary look.

I have enjoyed taking the finishing of each project to a point that reproduces, as best I can tell, that of the original piece as closely as possible; perhaps you will too. Some of the pieces are painted much as they would have been a couple of hundred years ago; some are finished with stain and little more than an oil or polyurethane finish; almost all are given a well-worn antique appearance through distressing, depending upon the piece, and the application of an antiquing glaze.

Pine lends itself readily to special treatments. It takes stain well, is close grained and so needs no filling, but the knots do tend to bleed. This can cause real problems, especially where white or light finishes are concerned. You'll need to use an inhibitor such as Kilz to stop the staining, or you can use a homemade pickling glaze such as the one described on page 24.

While each individual technique is described here, many are intermingled. That being so, you'll find a short, step-by-step finishing instruction in each chapter. These are not repeats of what follows, simply ways to apply and adjust a given technique, or techniques, to suit the piece.

RESULTS OF AGING

The older the piece, the smoother it will be, *everywhere*. Remember this all through the building and finishing process. Time and use tend to smooth rough surfaces, especially those that rub together or are handled often. Drawer tops, bottoms and runners will all have been worn smooth; corners will have been rounded over, some only ever so slightly; finishes will, in some instances, have been worn almost to nothing, especially around door edges, pulls and knobs; paint will have cracked, flaked, worn through; deep depressions will have been worn into work tops and so on. So, judicious sanding is required.

SANDING

Pine, as we all know, is a softwood and, if you're used to working only with hardwoods, you'll be amazed at the rate your sander will remove material; be very careful until you're used to working with this softer medium.

As soft as it is, you won't need to use the finest grade papers; 150 grit is about as fine as you'll need to go—anything finer is a waste of time and effort. The paper soon loads up and is rendered useless. By the same token, 80 grit is as coarse as you can go. Anything coarser will remove material at an alarming and often uncontrollable rate. I find 120 grit to be the answer to almost every situation. Rarely do I use anything else.

Most of your basic sanding should be done as you work through the project. I find sanding to be a tedious process and don't like to do it all at once. Also, some sections will need to be sanded before assembly.

Be sure to get all the end grains that will show; the better you sand them, the better they will take stain and finish. Sand the bottoms and sides of drawers. Sand the edges and tops of all doors and trim.

SHEEN

You'll find this mentioned many times throughout this book. Rarely do I use it as a stand-alone finish, more as a protective coat, a sealer, that's applied at various stages of the finishing process—often after each step. In the main, I use water-based satin or semigloss polyurethane for this step, but you can use whatever you prefer. Polyurethane also provides a hard coat that will give some protection against fine sanding during various stages of the distressing process.

WOOD COLOR/STAINING

Pine takes on a patina with time. It's the result of long years of exposure to light, air, dust, waxing and cleaning. It's a color that's difficult to describe, and differs from white pine to yellow pine. It can be a lovely buttery color, a deep bronze, even a deep shade of gold. If the piece has been waxed for many years it may have turned brown. If it's been scrubbed with soap and water it will be grayish white. It could even be almost black with age. Anywhere the wood will show, be it a natural finish or simply exposure due to time and wear, that patina should show; the wood should look old. This can only be achieved over a long period of time or by applying a stain.

Staining can be done in two stages: shelves and interior surfaces can be done before assembly; exterior surfaces should be done after distressing so that some of the stain will accumulate in the dings and scrapes. Several shades will work, but the ones I prefer are Provincial, Early American and Puritan Pine, all by Minwax, and Bleached Mahogany by Blond-it.

Method: Simply wipe the stain on, then wipe it off immediately and leave it to dry. Only when it's dry will you be able to see the true color. I am a great believer in multiple coats rather than leaving stain on for an indeterminate length of time. This gives me much more control over the final color. If you need to apply more than one coat, be sure the first coat is dry before applying the next. Do not leave the stain to dry before wiping; if you do you'll be left with a layer of scum that's difficult to remove. Remember, the older the piece, the deeper (darker) the color.

Finally, you'll need to apply a coat of sheen to seal and protect the stain. Often you'll want to rub through the subsequent layers of finish to reveal the wood, which will, of course, show the patina of time. If you rub through the stain and reveal new wood, the effect is destroyed; a coat of sheen will help to protect against this.

DISTRESSING

Almost all old pieces will have suffered the ravages of time and use and, if you're going for an authentic old-world look, you'll have to apply the effects of perhaps a couple of hundred years in less than a couple of hours. This is done quite easily using a minimum of readily available tools: a nice piece of rock weighing perhaps a couple of pounds, a bunch of old keys, a fairly heavy rasp file, a small hammer and a pound or two of mixed gravel—the pieces should be from ¼″ to ½″ in size and a mixture of rough and smooth pebbles.

Distressing is a subjective technique. What looks good to one can look terrible to another. The watchword is *restraint*. This is definitely one part of the finishing process where less is more, especially where finer pieces of furniture are concerned. Pieces in heavy use areas of the home, such as family rooms, kitchens and halls, will show more signs of wear and tear than pieces kept in more formal areas—drawing rooms, dining rooms, etc. Don't rush in and beat the piece up. When the time comes, stand back, sit down, survey the piece and think it through. Where would you expect it to show signs of wear? The drawing on page 110 will give you some ideas, but don't take it as gospel; it's meant only as a guideline. You'll find more suggestions listed along with construction notes throughout the book.

Methods of Distressing

Distressing should be done before staining. After spending so much time and effort building and sanding your fine piece of furniture, you'll find it more than a little traumatic when the time comes to apply the hammer,

so to speak. And it seems a little incongruous to spend lots of time sanding a piece to perfection and then taking a rock to it. Don't worry. If you do it right you can only enhance the piece. Regard distressing simply as one more part of the construction process.

Most problems with distressing come from over-enthusiasm; don't get carried away. It's difficult to know when or where to stop. Just remember this: Unless they are very old or have been badly mistreated, most pieces will show only slight signs of wear. People have always tended to look after their possessions, especially expensive furniture.

First, think it through.

Apply the rasp sparingly to exposed edges and sharp corners, which need to be slightly rounded with time. Be extremely careful when doing this. The tool can make deep gouges and we're looking only for timeworn scrapes.

Again using the rasp, tap the exposed edges here and there with the sharp edge. Don't overdo it; six dings are a lot.

Apply the edge of the hammer, gently here and there, not more than a half-dozen times to work tops and edges. Do the same with the rock.

Use the keys to make a few nicks and dings on work surfaces, trim and doors. Finally, stand back and throw a small handful of gravel, rough and smooth, at the piece. Not too hard. What's needed is only a hint of a mark.

Now quit; you've done enough, probably too much, already.

Note: Painted finishes require an extra step in the distressing process—see "Painted Finishes" this page.

ANTIQUING

This is the technique you'll use to add all those years. It's the penultimate step in the finishing process, and is applied to almost every piece just before the final coat of finish. It's nothing more than a dark, translucent glaze that's wiped or brushed on and then quickly wiped off again, leaving only a thin film, barely discernible, to approximate the layers of dirt and grime that accumulate over long periods of time. Why not simply rub the piece with dirt and dust, you might say? Well you could, but nine times out of ten, all you'll end up with is a dirty, grimy piece that looks just terrible. Antiquing is a subtle process, the effects of which should be apparent but not noticeable. Done properly, antiquing will add charm and authenticity to your piece. Remember all those

dings and scrapes you made during the distressing process? These will be enhanced by the antiquing oil. Residue of the oil will remain in them after you've wiped the bulk of it off, looking just like the accumulated grime of centuries—neat.

Recipe: There are a couple of options here. First: To one quart of paint thinner (not lacquer thinner) add one ounce each of burnt sienna and burnt umber pigment and mix thoroughly; this is a wipe-on, wipe-off oil. Better is the glaze I use: Take one pint of water-based polyurethane, thin it one-to-one with water, add enough pigment—two to three teaspoons of powder or two to three tablespoons of poster paint—to make a transparent glaze.

Method: Apply the oil or glaze over a prior coat of sheen. If you're using the oil version, take two rags, one in each hand. Dip one in the antiquing oil and wipe it onto the piece, then immediately wipe it off again using the dry rag in the other hand. The oil dries very quickly, so don't wait before wiping it off. Leave it on too long and you'll have a real mess on your hands. When you've done all the exposed areas, let the piece stand for a while—an hour should do nicely—then apply a final coat of sheen.

If you're using the poly glaze, you can brush it on, then if necessary use a balled-up cloth to remove the excess. Remember, a thin film is all that's required. When the glaze is dry, cover it with a final coat of satin or semigloss sheen.

PAINTED FINISHES

Most early American and English everyday furniture, especially that used in kitchens or family rooms, was painted for a number of reasons: to protect and beautify it, to match the overall decor of a room or to make an inexpensive wood look like another (grain painting). Yet rarely today will you see an old piece with its original paint. This is because, during the early part of the twentieth century, refinishing antique furniture was the vogue. Almost all painted pieces were stripped, scrubbed and given a look they never had, much to the exasperation of today's collector. Old pieces with even a vestige of their original painted finish are highly prized. Scrubbed pine was found only where water was present—in the kitchen.

From the beginning of the seventeenth century, red, black and yellow were the colors of choice. By the turn of the eighteenth century almost any color you can think of was used, but especially red, black, green, brown, gray and white; blue didn't become popular until the nineteenth century, and the subtle shades rendered by the now much discussed milk paints probably did not appear until after 1825.

So, bear all this in mind when considering a painted finish. If you're trying for an authentic eighteenth-century look, you won't want to paint your piece blue. Then again, if you're simply looking for a pleasing effect with an aged look, it really doesn't matter what color you use.

Red was often used as a base coat, and many of the painted finishes described in this book follow that tradition, especially where the base coat is destined to show through the top coat.

Often a piece was painted over and over. Often, to some degree or another, each of those coats will show somewhere, which leads me to mention another step in the distressing process. Paint, more than any other finish, shows the toll of time and use. It will have been worn through, layer after layer, by the constant rubbing of hands, clothing, utensils, pots, pans, dishes, etc., and your piece should show similar abrading. Once again, don't overdo it. Edges of doors, trim, drawers, rails and large areas on work tops will all show signs—and the operative word is *signs*—of wear and tear. This is achieved by gently rubbing through the layers, carefully and selectively. The best time to do this is when the paint is around twenty-four hours old, assuming you're using latex or acrylic paint. Take a small piece of wet-and-dry sandpaper of at least 400 grit, soak it thoroughly (and keep it wet) and very gently rub the chosen area. Now, keep a close watch on what you're doing. The wearing away happens quickly and is difficult to see through the sludge and colored water, which hides progress. Wipe often and look closely. Often you'll want to show only a hint of what lies below. Sometimes you'll want to go through layer after layer, all the way to the stain. Again, care is essential. Even with a coat of sheen, it takes little pressure to go right through to the raw wood below. Do this and you have a real problem on your hands. This step in the distressing process is fun to do, and the results, provided you've not gone too far, are very pleasing.

Old paint will often be crackled—sometimes called alligatored—due to the different consistencies in each layer; one shrinking a little more than another as it ages. How to achieve this look is described on page 20 under "Crackling."

Color, as with any other old finish, becomes muted with time—thus the need once more for antiquing oil.

What type of paint will you use? Milk paints are available from various supply houses, but they are not appropriate for all pieces. They do a great job, so I'm told, but I've never used them. Instead, I prefer to use modern, water-based, latex or acrylic house paints. I like the quick-drying properties, easy cleanup and lack of odor. And they're easy to work once they're dry.

APPLYING FINISHES

First, remember all old painted finishes were applied by hand, often by someone who wasn't too bothered about a professional look. This means brush marks and runs here and there. Don't worry too much if you, too, have a run or two; the effect will simply provide a little more authenticity.

I don't own any spraying equipment. That's not to say I wouldn't like to. But, then again, time spent mixing paints and cleaning equipment can be better spent doing other things. Many people say you can't do a decent paint job unless you spray; not true. I apply everything with a brush, even stains. However, use whichever method you feel most comfortable with. I own a half-dozen expensive bristle and nylon brushes, and I buy foam/poly brushes by the case. I use natural bristle brushes for oil-based paints and synthetic bristles for latex and acrylic mediums. This is because water causes natural bristles to swell. Use a good brush and you can lay the paint down very nicely, better, I think, than you can with a spray gun; thicker, for sure. Even so, you'll often need at least two coats to cover properly, especially when using dark colors. A good brush is an investment; a cheap brush is an expense.

What's a good brush? Apart from it costing $30 to $40, the bristles on a good brush, natural or synthetic, should all be tapered and "flagged," split at the tips to form tiny forks. Even on the best brushes, however, all the bristles may not be split, but the more the better. Hold the brush up to the light and separate the bristles; you should be able to see the splits. Compare several brushes; you'll find one may have more flags than another. That's the one you want. The bristles should also have a definite spring to them, and they should taper to a chisel edge at the tip. Start out with a 3″ brush. It will do most jobs, and you can add other sizes as your budget may allow.

CRACKLING

Time, like it does with everything else, takes its toll on paint. Over the years it dries out, loses its resilience, shrinks and cracks—crackles. With a little practice you can reproduce this effect. Done properly, I think, crackling produces a very attractive and authentic look. It's also an effect that can be done to a greater or lesser degree. A very light crackle, a mere crazing of the surface, creates a very subtle look; heavy crackling, however, produces a stark, even startling effect. It depends on the piece and what you feel most comfortable with. Today you can buy this effect in a can. Some hardware stores and a few mail-order supply houses carry it. You simply spray it on and voilà. It's easy and quick. I prefer to do it by hand and by degree, however. It's more fun, and you end up with not only a great look but also with a real sense of achievement. So, how's it done?

Method: First, put a little thought into what color will lie on top of another. In other words, what will show through the top coat? One of the nicest examples I have ever seen of this technique was on a very large conference table; it wasn't more than a year old, but looked much older. It was done in black on red. The crackling had been done sparingly, only around the edges of the top, and the cracks were very fine. The surface had been rubbed and polished to a high shine. Green on red looks good. Black on white does not. Think it through.

Second, use water-based paints.

You'll also need some liquid hide glue—I use Franklin's—which you'll need to thin with water to a brushable consistency; it doesn't take much thinning, about one part water to three parts glue, perhaps a little more.

You'll need to apply stain, a coat of sheen to protect it as you rub through the various layers and then your base coat. You'll not need more than one coat of base color as coverage doesn't matter too much; very little of it will show. Next, apply another coat of sheen, again to protect the base coat. Now brush on the glue. You can completely cover the piece, or you can apply it sparingly and selectively. It's just a matter of taste. For even greater control I sometimes apply and spread the glue with my fingertips, pushing and squeezing the glue—thinner in one place, thicker in another. Now allow the piece to stand for twenty-four hours until the glue dries completely. The next step is the one you should practice. Don't attempt it on the real thing until you've tried it several times on pieces of scrap board. I find it best to do this step in stages. I turn the piece and paint each

Apply one coat of stain.

Apply water-based polyurethane.

Apply one coat of base paint.

surface on the horizontal. This prevents the paint from falling when it reacts with the glue. The way you apply the paint is critical. Load the brush, take a deep breath and lay the paint down using one, two or three very quick, lightning-short sweeps—no more than six to eight inches—back and forth, before the glue has time to react. Be careful as you move along the piece; overlaps are danger areas. There's no easy way to do this step, and your first attempts will be less than perfect. I have no doubt that your brushstrokes will not be quick enough. The effect—the reaction of the paint on the glue—is almost instantaneous, and, if you're not fast enough, the second sweep of the brush will have a disastrous effect that must be seen rather than described. You must completely cover the base coat, or at least as best you can; a few thin spots won't matter. You won't be able to apply a second coat, even after the first is dry; the glue will continue to react to water. This is,

perhaps, the one area where a spray gun can do a better job, but only marginally so.

Once the paint is completely dry you have a couple of options: You can do some selective rubbing down or you can simply apply a coat of sheen, another of antiquing oil and then a final coat of sheen.

When the paint is completely dry I like to rub the surface smooth before applying the final coat of satin sheen. You'll also need to show all the signs of age, rubbing through the various layers where natural wear and tear would take place: outer edges, trim, doors, feet, etc. The rubbing down should be done with wet-and-dry sandpaper of at least 400 grit or even 0000 steel wool. *Do not use water.* Water will react with the glue and you'll have a mess on your hands. I use paint thinner. Keep the paper or steel wool wet, and take great care.

Apply liquid hide glue.

Apply top coat of paint.

Rub through outer coats.

Apply antiquing oil and polyurethane.

THE PEELING PAINT EFFECT

All painted finishes tend to strip and peel with age. I often wondered how to achieve this look, but couldn't figure it out until I did it by accident one day not so long ago when I was in a hurry to finish a particular piece. It happened when I didn't allow enough time for the layers to fully cure between the steps. Here's how it's done:

The first step is to apply *two* coats of semigloss polyurethane over the base coat of stain and allow them to fully cure for about twenty-four hours.

The next two steps take time and speed. That seems to be something of a contradiction, but you'll see what I mean. First, apply two or three coats of flat latex or acrylic paint over the polyurethane, or however many it takes to completely cover the stain. *You must apply each coat before the previous one is completely cured.* As you apply each coat, wait only long enough for the previous coat to become touch dry, then apply the next.

Again, while the paint is still soft, say after waiting an hour, you'll need to do the initial rubbing down. Using 220-grit wet-and-dry and a lot of water, start rubbing the paint along the direction of the grain. Apply more pressure than you usually would. The still-soft paint will begin to pull away from the slick finish below. Do this to a greater or lesser degree as may please you best; in this case, however, more is better.

After you've achieved the right degree of stripping for your taste, allow the paint to fully cure, maybe for as long as forty-eight hours.

Now you'll need to apply any appropriate wear and tear. Using 320-grit wet-and-dry and a lot of water, wear away the paint to the polyurethane coats below, but don't go through them. If you show bare new wood, you'll spoil the entire finish. Also, be careful and rub down using only light pressure; the paint may still tend to strip.

Finally, apply a light film of antiquing glaze and seal the finish with a couple of coats of satin polyurethane.

GRAIN/VINEGAR PAINTING

Grain-painted furniture is very desirable today. I don't necessarily mean one type of wood painted to look like another, more a decorative effect in the trompe l'oeil style. This finish was popular in the late eighteenth and early nineteenth centuries, and the patterns were achieved in a number of ways using different mediums and tools: fingers, feathers, brushes, sponges, combs,

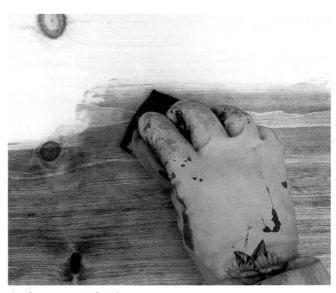

Apply one coat of stain.

Apply two coats of gloss polyurethane.

Rub paint until it begins to lift.

crumpled paper, even candle smoke. Done properly, the appearance is often spectacular and well worth the effort. The process requires a tinted glaze applied over a solid base coat, which is then marked in some way while still wet. It's a finish that's great fun to do, but also one that requires practice.

Materials: Latex or acrylic base coat, glaze and an applicator of some sort—finger, brush, feather, etc.

The Glaze: You'll need some light corn syrup, distilled white vinegar and powdered pigment or poster paints. Add two teaspoons of corn syrup to four teaspoons of powdered pigment or poster paint and mix well until you have a smooth paste. Now add eight teaspoons of vinegar and mix thoroughly.

Method: Apply the base coat; it should be a strong color, preferably one of the earth tones. Make sure the coverage is complete—apply a second coat if necessary—and allow it to dry thoroughly. Next, apply the glaze to a small but complete section of the piece, a section you can work over a period of fifteen or twenty minutes. It should be applied thinly so that it's smooth and semitransparent. It's best not to do this step on a humid or damp day. While the glaze is still wet, make the pattern by pressing and smearing lightly with your finger, dragging a feather, scraping with a comb or pressing with crumpled plastic wrap or a sponge; be creative. If you mess up or if the glaze dries before you've finished, don't worry. Simply start over by brushing the section with a little vinegar and the surface will be ready to rework. When the work is complete, allow the glaze to dry thoroughly. This won't take long, usually about an hour. Now apply a couple of coats of polyurethane (not water-based).

Apply one or two base coats.

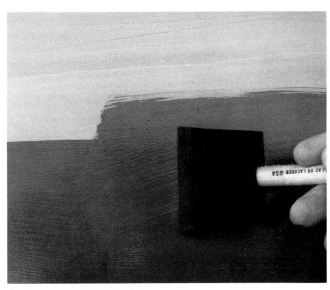
Apply a generous coat of glaze.

You'll need: white vinegar, light corn syrup, powdered pigment, water-based paint and an applicator (a potato).

Place and lift applicator for pattern

PICKLING

Not pickling in the true sense of the word, this is another painted finish, easy to do and very effective.

The conventional method is to simply thin water- or oil-based paints to a consistency that allows the underlying grain, knots, etc., to show through, even when two or more coats are applied. Unfortunately, pine has a tendency to bleed around the knots, creating yellow stains that look terrible, especially when the pickle is white. This means you'll have to apply a sealer: Kilz, or some such. This bothered me a great deal until I came up with a simple solution. Instead of thinning my paint with water, I use a water-based satin polyurethane, about one part paint to one part poly, and I apply it directly to the untreated wood, both as a sealer and finish. This does not actually make for a thinner paint, simply a thinner pigment. It seems to work well and, to date, I have had no complaints about bleeding. Certainly none of the pieces I've kept show any signs of it.

Method: Choose your color, mix the water-based paint and polyurethane one-to-one or even thinner if you prefer. Then apply directly to the surface with a foam brush, wiping it off again as you go. This will stain rather than paint the surface, leaving all the underlying knots and grain to show through. You'll need to sand the grain before applying a second coat. I like to apply at least two coats, sometimes three, always wiping as I go and allowing each coat to dry before applying the next. Once I have achieved the desired effect I stop, allow the final coat to dry thoroughly, rub the surface smooth with 250-grit paper, then apply a coat of Minwax Antiquing Oil (not to be confused with aging oil described earlier) which can be buffed within ten minutes or so and gives the piece a nice luster.

BLEACHING

Bleaching is a fairly simple process. It's best done on pieces that would have been used in or around the kitchen: kitchen tables, bucket stands, etc. Any of the proprietary brands of bleach will work.

Method: Remove all traces of oil, grease and glue. Wear rubber gloves and apply a generous coat of undiluted bleach. Allow it to dry, then neutralize it by washing the piece with clean, warm water. It shouldn't take more than one coat to achieve the right look, but if it does simply repeat the process. After neutralizing, allow the piece to stand for a couple of days to allow any residual chemicals to escape. If not, they may cause the

Using a rag for a grain painting.

Don't use water-based polyurethane to finish vinegar painting.

Apply heavy coat of pickling mixture.

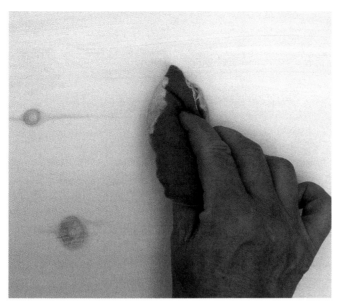
Wipe off most pickling mix.

finishing coats to blister. Never leave a bleached surface any longer than two days without finishing; it will soon begin to darken again. Now apply a couple of coats of blonde shellac (more about this later). Allow that to harden overnight, then rub it lightly along the grain with some 0000 steel wool. Finally, you can apply a couple of coats of wax polish or Minwax Antiquing Oil. Allow that to harden—overnight for the wax, ten minutes or so for the Minwax—then buff with a clean soft cloth.

SCRUBBED FINISH

This is a method you can use to achieve the appearance that only comes when an old piece of pine furniture has been stripped of its paint.

Method: Don't try this until you've practiced it on several pieces of scrap stock and achieved a look that pleases you. Start by applying a stain to give the piece some semblance of patina: Early American, Bleached Mahogany, Provincial, etc. Don't overdo it. It shouldn't be too dark. I find it best to wipe it on with a rag barely dampened with stain after I've done my distressing. Next, take some cream latex or acrylic paint; it should be a good solid cream. Mix this one-to-one—even thinner, if you like a more subtle effect—with satin polyurethane. Brush the mixture on generously, wiping it off almost immediately as you go, leaving no more than a thin, somewhat patchy film that should approximate the desired effect. Rub the surface with a pad of 0000 steel wool to cut the raised grain until it's silky smooth. Now you can cover the piece with a couple of coats of clear polyurethane; satin is best for a natural look.

SHELLAC/FRENCH POLISH

Shellac is an old-world finish still used today, but rarely applied as it was by the old masters. It is, perhaps, the best of sealers, and other finishes can be applied over the top of it. French polishing with shellac as it was done by the old masters has almost died away; done properly, however, it is a very exciting finish. To do it right requires dedication and hard work. It's a tedious process, but the results are well worth all the effort.

You can buy shellac ready mixed as a liquid, usually as a three-pound cut, or you can buy the raw flakes and mix it yourself, which is the method I prefer. For reproduction antiques you'll need one of the less refined shellacs, such as seedlac, buttonlac or garnetlac. These need straining before use but produce a nice range of tones from brown to amber. Orange and blonde shellacs do not need to be strained and in some cases you may need to use one of these, too.

The cut, as you probably already know, refers to the mixture: one pound of flakes to one gallon of denatured alcohol is a one-pound cut. You'll never mix a gallon at a time; two ounces to a pint (about four tablespoons to a cup-and-a-quarter) works nicely as a one-pound cut; four ounces (eight tablespoons) per pint makes a two-pound cut; six ounces (twelve tablespoons) makes a three-pound cut and so on.

Method: Mixing—Put the flakes into a glass container—a large jelly jar with a tight-fitting lid will do fine—then add the alcohol. Put the lid on and allow the mixture to stand for several hours, stirring occasionally, until the flakes are completely dissolved. If you've used one of the shellacs that need straining, pour it through a paint filter then return it to the jar; it's now ready to use.

First you'll need to do any necessary staining and distressing.

For sealing, a one-pound cut will do fine. Simply apply a coat with a natural bristle brush, wait for it to dry, about forty-five minutes, then lightly sand.

To use shellac as a finish a three-pound cut is best; it's easier going with two-pound, but you'll need to apply more coats. Shellac sets up quite quickly so you'll have to work fast. Using a natural bristle brush, apply your first coat, allow it to dry, then sand lightly with 180-grit sandpaper. Apply two or three more coats leaving each one to dry overnight. There should be no need to sand between coats. The second coat will dissolve and mix with the first to form a single, thick coat and so on. However, before you apply each subsequent coat you should inspect the previous one; you may find a run or two. These can be taken off with 180-grit sandpaper. When you've applied the final coat and it's dried thoroughly, take a piece of 400-grit wet-and-dry—you might go as fine as 600-grit if you like—and dampen it with linseed oil, then gently rub the entire surface. Finally, remove the residue of the oil by gently wiping the surface with a soft cloth barely dampened with alcohol. You should now have a finish to be proud of. If you've distressed lightly and used one of the darker shellacs, you'll be amazed at what you've achieved.

French polishing requires a one-pound cut and some real dedication on your part. First sand the piece smooth, do any necessary distressing and apply a non-grain-raising stain of an appropriate color. Then take a soft, lint-free cloth, roll it into a ball and dip it into the shellac. Now rub the shellac onto the wood using fast, straight strokes along the grain. After the first coat has dried, about forty-five minutes to an hour, lightly sand using 600-grit paper. Continue to add coats, lightly sanding between each one, until the finish begins to glow. Now add eight to ten drops of boiled linseed oil to the shellac, mix well and apply another coat, this time rubbing in a circular motion. Continue to add more coats, adding a little more oil to the shellac with each one, until a deep, glowing finish is achieved. You'll need to apply at least eight coats, perhaps as many as a dozen or even more, but the results are well worth all the effort.

SHOP TIP
Containers for Finishing Products

Microwave/dishwasher-safe food storage containers—4½"-cup size—make great containers for holding all sorts of odds and ends of finish: beeswax, shellac, paint, antiquing glaze, etc. You can buy them from discount stores for 50 or 75 cents each. They are airtight, easy to clean, long lasting and stackable. Some even have places on the sides where you can write the contents and date.

BEESWAX

Beeswax is easy to prepare. Take a small cake—I buy mine at Ace Hardware for $1.29 a cake—and break it into small pieces. Put the pieces into a glass dish, add just enough turpentine to barely cover them, then leave the mixture to soak. When the beeswax has absorbed the turpentine it's ready to use. Simply roll it into a ball; wrap the ball in a piece of lint-free cloth; twist the ends of the cloth so the wax is squeezed through the cloth and run the ball over the finish in a circular motion. Now buff to a shine.

OTHER FINISHES

There are finishes, other than those described above, used on various pieces throughout this book. They are, for the most part, simple and easy to apply; you'll find them described in the appropriate places.

Chapter 4

Nineteenth-Century Butler's Tea Table

I t's not been that long since every great house, and many not so great, both in England and America, had a butler. Some of them still do. In the domestic hierarchy the butler was at the top. He was in charge of running the house as well as being the first line of communication between the family and its servant staff. He also looked after most of the family's needs, organizing menus, cleaning and supervising the daily routine

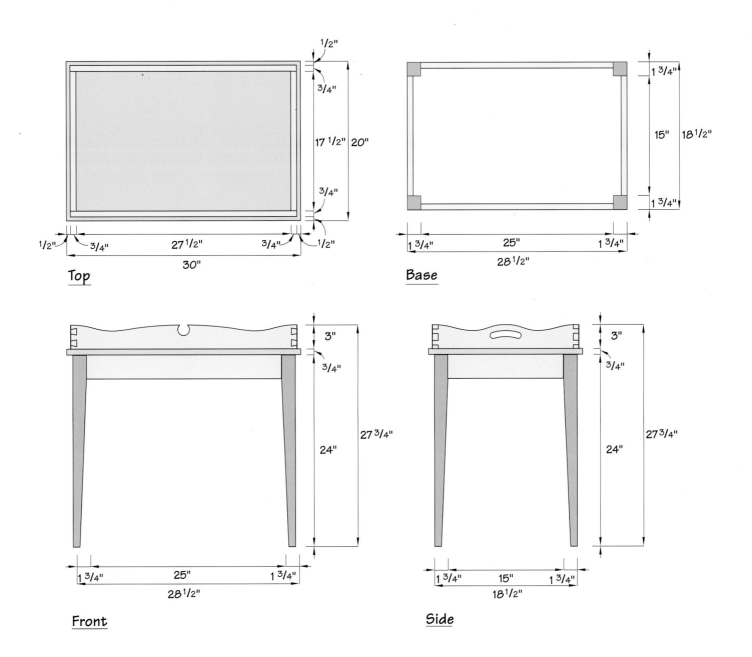

Top

Base

Front

Side

of the upstairs staff. His world was run from what was known as the butler's pantry—not a pantry in the true sense of the word, more a small office. He waited upon the family's every need, bringing the daily newspaper to the master of the house in the morning and serving all the formal meals—breakfast, lunch, dinner and, of course, afternoon tea. Afternoon tea in England, and to a lesser extent in America, was and still is a very important part of the day, especially among the upper class where it was always served by the butler. Afternoon tea was something of a ritual, taken casually in the parlor or, on fine days, outside on the lawns among the flowers.

A tenoning jig is great for making quick, accurate tenons. You set the depth of cut for the blade, the position of the jig support plate, run the cut on one side, reverse the piece and run it again, and then flip the piece end over and repeat the process.

Set the depth of cut for your table saw blade to remove the waste and reveal the cheeks of the joint, and then, if your table saw has a movable rip fence, set it as a stop so you can make a consistently accurate shoulder cut. If not, you'll need to use a sacrifice fence.

It consisted of a pot of tea, small sandwiches and tea cakes, often scones and jam. All this was brought to the family either on a large tray placed on a low table or a tray with legs of its own—a tea table.

The earliest tea tables were simply that, small tables. Later they incorporated a low gallery pierced with handle holes. Those made around the middle to late nineteenth century had hinged sides, also pierced with handle holes, that stopped the goodies sliding off when the piece was being carried, but dropped flat when the journey from below stairs was complete, thus increasing the size of the tabletop.

It's the latter design you're probably familiar with and certainly see most often. Few of the earlier versions survived the centuries.

The early version of the butler's tea table was quite an elegant piece. Some had turned legs, some square and straight and some tapered. The gallery also took many forms. Some were no more than a rail that extended all around the edge of the tabletop, the piece being carried by placing the hands around the edges. Others were quite ornate. Ours incorporates the best of both worlds.

WHAT'S IT WORTH?

I've seen tables like this for sale in fine stores for $400 and up. The cost of materials is less than $10, so it can be something of a money spinner. I sell mine to the trade for $95, which is very profitable since I can make as many as four in a single day.

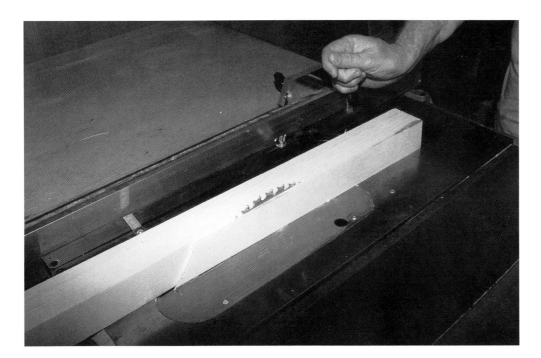

Use your tapering jig to cut the tapers to the legs. If you don't have one, it's a relatively simple job to make one.

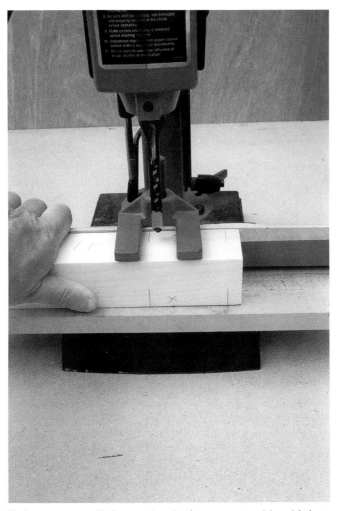

To be sure you mill the mortises in the correct position, it's best to lay out the legs before you start, and then mark the position of each mortise and each leg as left front, right front and so on.

CONSTRUCTION OUTLINE

This fairly simple project can easily be completed over a weekend. The construction for the legs and apron is mortise and tenon. The top is fastened to the understructure with screws in pocket holes. The gallery is fastened to the top also with screws. The gallery is constructed using dovetail joints at the corners, and the legs, being nicely tapered, are very much in the style of Hepplewhite.

BUILDING THE TABLE

STEP 1. Cut all the pieces to size.

STEP 2. Build the board for the top.

STEP 3. Using either the jointer, as I do, or the table saw and beginning 6″ from the top, cut the tapers to two adjacent sides of each of the four legs. Be sure to cut two left- and two right-hand. The taper is roughly 2°.

STEP 4. Cut mortises 2″ long × ⅜″ wide × 1″ deep to the tops of the tapered sides of all four legs. Set the mortises ½″ from the top of the leg.

STEP 5. Mill tenons 2″ long × ⅜″ wide × 1″ deep to the ends of all four pieces of the apron.

STEP 6. Dry assemble the pieces together to make sure you have a good fit, then disassemble them again.

STEP 7. Mill through dovetails to the ends of all four pieces that will make up the gallery.

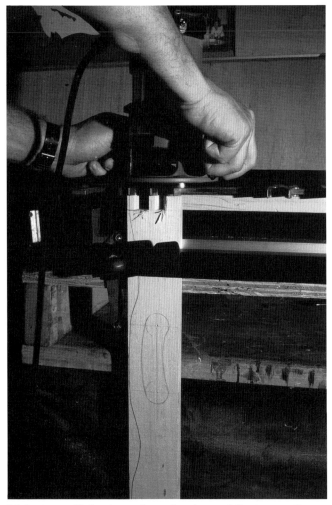

It's best to mill the dovetails to the pieces of the tray section before you cut out the details.

STEP 8. Dry assemble the gallery to make sure you have a good fit—the joints should be tight allowing for little or no movement between the pieces.

STEP 9. Disassemble the gallery and, using the pattern, cut the detail and handle slots to the gallery.

STEP 10. Sand all the parts smooth and break all sharp edges.

STEP 11. Apply an appropriate stain (I used Jacobean by Minwax) to all of the parts.

STEP 12. Glue, assemble and clamp the understructure and leave it overnight to completely cure.

STEP 13. Glue, assemble and clamp the gallery and leave it overnight to cure.

STEP 14. From underneath, using six no. $6 \times 1\frac{5}{8}''$ screws—two along each side and one at each end—fasten the gallery to the top. You should elongate the holes slightly to allow the top to breathe.

STEP 15. Mill six pocket holes to the upper inside edges of the understructure's apron. If you have a drill press you do this before you do the assembly (see drawing and photo).

STEP 16. Assemble the top to the understructure.

FINISHING

No big surprises here. I simply apply a half-dozen coats of seedlac over a couple of days and it's done.

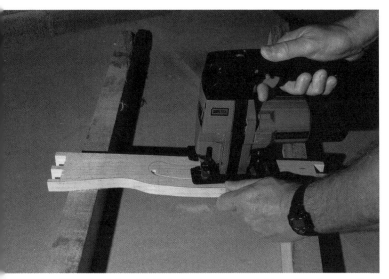

To cut out the details to the handles and sides of the tray section, raise the pieces by using a couple of pieces of 2×4, and then use your jigsaw to remove the waste.

Chapter 5

Eighteenth-Century Oval Tavern Table

O ne of the most important institutions, both in Europe and Colonial America, was the inn or tavern. It was, and in Europe still is, the social center of the community. But it was more than just a gathering place. It was the place to get up-to-date news, where politics were discussed and town meetings were held. It was also the scene of hard drinking and rowdiness, and the furniture therein was built to withstand

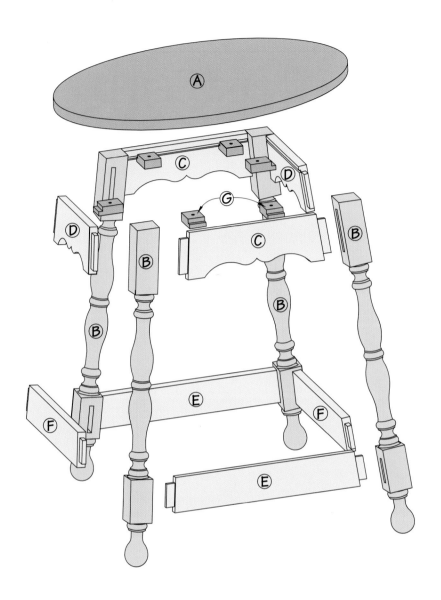

SHOP TIP
Marking an Oval

On your 27″ × 25″ plywood, mark a line down the center of the length. Mark the middle of the center line, then measure out 6¼″ to either side and mark both spots. Drive a small screw partway into each of the two spots, leaving the head proud by about ⅛″. Now take a piece of thin string, double it in two and make a loop 19¼″ in diameter; it doesn't need to be exact, ⅛″ either way won't matter. Next take a pencil, lay the string around the two screws as you see in photo on page 36, place the pencil inside the loop and draw the string tight. Now, keeping the string tight, push the pencil around the oval, which should finish roughly 26″ × 23″. Finally, cut the oval from the rectangle, adhering closely to the line, and sand the edge smooth and true.

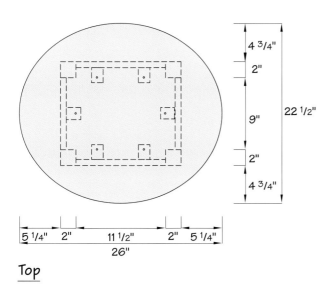

Top

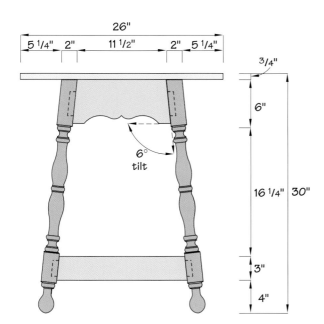

Side

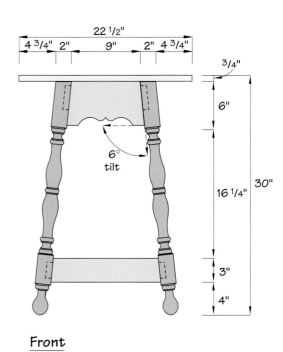

Front

MATERIALS LIST

Tavern Table

No.	Letter	Item	Dimensions T W L
1	A	Top	¾″ × 22½″ × 26″
4	B	Legs	2″ × 2″ × 29½″
2	C	Long Aprons	¾″ × 5½″ × 14½″
2	D	Short Aprons	¾″ × 5½″ × 12½″
2	E	Long Foot Rails	¾″ × 3″ × 18½″
2	F	Short Foot Rails	¾″ × 3″ × 16¼″
6	G	Buttons	¾″ × 1½″ × 2¼″

inevitable abuse. So, tavern tables, in one form or another, have been around for centuries, but were at their most popular during the eighteenth and nineteenth centuries. Typically they had square, rectangular, round, octagonal or, in rare cases, oval tops, and three or four tapered, square or turned, splayed legs. (It seems square legs didn't appear until after 1790, before that they were all turned.) Antique oval tables were and are quite rare. This one is typical of those made in New England from 1700 until 1820. The turned legs are typical of the late Jacobean–early Queen Anne period. It's an elegant piece, unusual and will definitely be a nice addition to your home.

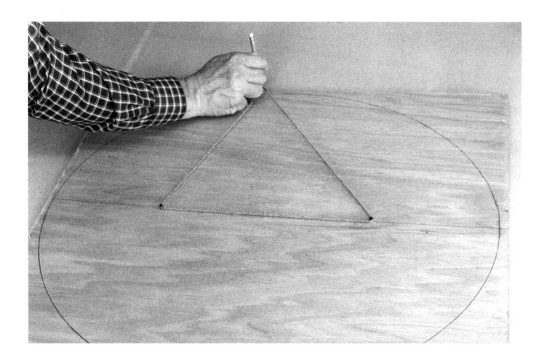

This setup will provide the oval shape for the tabletop (see Shop Tip on page 34).

WHAT'S IT WORTH?

I sold mine to the trade for $195—not bad for a weekend's fun in the shop and less than $20 in materials—and received orders for more.

CONSTRUCTION OUTLINE

At first look, this seems a fairly simple piece, but one or two tricky areas present something of a challenge. But it's fun to build, incorporates the two basic elements of furniture construction—turning and joinery—and you get to use almost every tool in the shop.

The legs, apron and rails are joined together with mortise and tenon joints, and the top is attached to the base with six buttons, but you can use cleats and screws or pockets if you like. The board for the top is constructed using three pieces of stock eight inches wide with the grain alternated for stability. The legs are turned from blanks cut from 2″ × 12″ stock. If you don't have a lathe, you can substitute tapered square legs. I cut the mortises in the legs using a dedicated hollow chisel machine; you can use hand tools. If you use a mortise machine or an attachment for your drill press, you may find that cutting mortises for left- and right-hand legs can be a little confusing. I use a piece of scrap stock, screwed to the bed on my machine, and mark the stop and start positions on it; you might like to do the same (see photo). The compound angles at the top of the legs and apron take a little figuring out, but you'll find instructions below. The ends of the rails that make up the apron are angled at 6° to provide the correct splay of the legs, and the tenons have to be angled upward at an angle of 6° to fit the mortises (see photo).

BUILDING THE TABLE

STEP 1. Cut all the pieces as laid out in the materials list, run them through the jointer and then cut the cyma curves to the lower edges of the four pieces that will make up the apron. Glue up the stock to make the top.

STEP 2. From a piece of ¼″ plywood 27″ × 25″ make a pattern for the top—see Shop Tip.

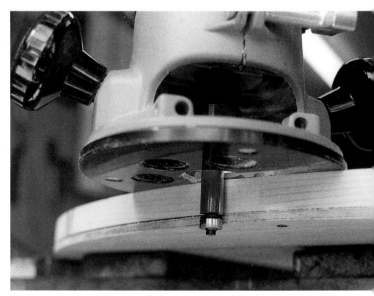

Use your plywood pattern and a ½″ flush trimming bit in your router to true the edge of the tabletop.

STEP 3. Use the pattern to mark an oval on the underside of the top.

STEP 4. Cut the oval ⅛″ larger than the mark.

STEP 5. Use small screws to attach the plywood pattern to the underside of the top, making sure excess material shows all around the oval.

STEP 6. Take your router and a flush trimming bit and trim the edge of the top true. Remove the pattern from the top.

STEP 7. Replace the flush trimming bit with a ¾″ round-over bit and round the top edge of the top.

STEP 8. Sand the top smooth and set it aside.

STEP 9. Take one of the leg blanks, mark the top and lower square sections and set it into your lathe.

STEP 10. Using a large gouge, round the section between the squares and the section beyond the lower square.

STEP 11. Mark for the beads, coves and ball foot as laid out in the drawing, turn to size and sand smooth.

STEP 12. Repeat the process for the other three legs using the first leg as a reference and marking aid.

STEP 13. Cut the mortises ¾″ deep in the legs—two left and two right—as per the drawing.

STEP 14. Set your table saw miter gauge to 6° off 90 and trim the ends of the apron and foot rails.

Attach a piece of scrap stock to the bed of your mortise machine or drill press, and mark the left- and right-hand start and finish positions. This ensures accurate positioning and makes it simple to work left- and right-hand legs.

STEP 15. Remove the guard from your table saw and set the blade to a depth of ¾″.

STEP 16. If you have a tenoning jig, set the back-stop to 6° off the vertical and cut the shoulders. **Note:** Do this first on a piece of scrap stock and test the tenon for fit in one of the mortises.

STEP 17. Mark the small shoulders at an angle of 6° (see

After cutting the rails to length and trimming the ends to an angle of 6°, set the back-stop on your tenoning jig to 6° and cut the tenons.

the photo) to accommodate the angle inside the mortise.

STEP 18. Use your band saw to cut the small shoulders.

STEP 19. Replace the guard on your table saw and tilt the blade to 6°.

STEP 20. Set your rip fence to 5½", lay the rails flat on the table, outer side up and top edge toward the blade, and trim the edge to 6° so that top of the understructure will fit flush to the underside of the top. Mark the outer top corner of each leg as you see in the photo at right.

STEP 21. Make a small jig (see photo below), return the table saw blade to 90°, set your miter gauge to 6° off 90 and, using the jig, trim the top of each leg. This is also so the top of the understructure will fit flush to the underside of the top.

STEP 22. Dry fit all the rails to the legs and lay the top on the structure; all should sit true.

STEP 23. Disassemble all the pieces, sand everything smooth, glue, reassemble the understructure, clamp and leave overnight to cure, but do not attach the top yet.

FINISHING

I did a little light distressing—just a small ding or two—before staining the pieces with Provincial by Minwax. Then I applied a sealer coat of shellac—seedlac at a one-

You'll need to cut the shoulders of the tenons to angle upward at 6° so they'll fit the mortises properly.

pound cut—and left it overnight to fully cure. Next, I lightly sanded the grain and applied four more coats of seedlac at a three-pound cut and rubbed the surface smooth with 0000 steel wool (see "Finishing," chapter three). This gave the piece a rich, dark luster. Next I assembled the top to the understructure and finished the whole thing off with a couple of coats of beeswax buffed to a shine.

Make this simple jig to trim the tops of the legs to an angle of 6°; note that the blade is vertical and that the miter gauge is set at 6°.

Chapter 6

Trestle Table

The trestle table as it was in Colonial times was a large, functional piece up to 12′ feet long by 24″ to 36″ wide supported by two or three heavy T-shaped trestles, hence the name. As you can imagine, it was a hefty piece—solid, substantial and probably the focus of whatever room in which it was placed. Each trestle rested on a blocklike foot, beveled from the ends to the upright, known as a shoe foot. Later, with the introduction of the cyma curve, the feet, cleats and legs became things of beauty. The trestles were connected by a single stretcher or rail that passed through mortises midway up from the floor. These were held in place by

wooden pegs. Tables like this became popular in the mid-1600s and were used mostly in the kitchens of large houses, in churches as communion tables and in other public buildings. They remain popular today, and the basic design has changed very little. The larger versions were made of oak; the smaller ones usually of pine (some had a pine top and a maple understructure). Smaller versions, often made on farms, measured four to six feet in length. Few originals have survived the centuries. Those that have are found mostly in museums. Ours is the farmhouse version—6′ long × 3′ wide × 30″ high.

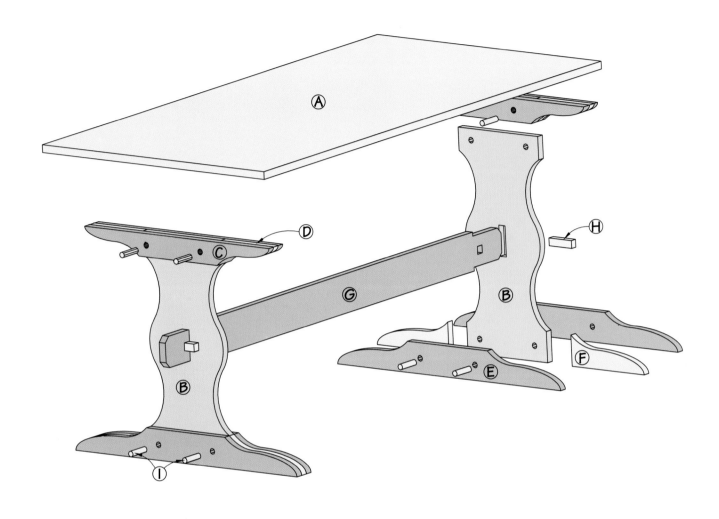

WHAT'S IT WORTH?

A table like this should easily fetch from $250 to $350 if you sell it to the trade. It could go for more if you sell it privately.

CONSTRUCTION OUTLINE

The table is made exclusively from furniture-grade pine. The top is made from three pieces of stock a full 1″ thick. The growth rings are alternated to ensure a more stable structure. The trestles and stretcher are made from the same 1″ stock. The cleats and feet employ extensive use of the cyma curve. Each is made from four pieces of stock, all 1″ thick, sandwiched together to make a solid base.

The method is straightforward and lends itself nicely to simple construction techniques. The construction of the feet and cleats provides ready-made mortises into which the legs tightly fit. The three pieces of stock that form the top are biscuited together, but you can use dowels if you prefer. The legs are cut from a single piece of stock 12″ wide × 1″ thick × 29″ long; again, the design of the legs makes good use of the cyma curve. The legs are set into the feet and cleats and held in place with ¾″ dowels, which are in turn permanently fixed in place with one of the new polyurethane glues. The top is attached to the legs using no. 10 × 3″ wood screws.

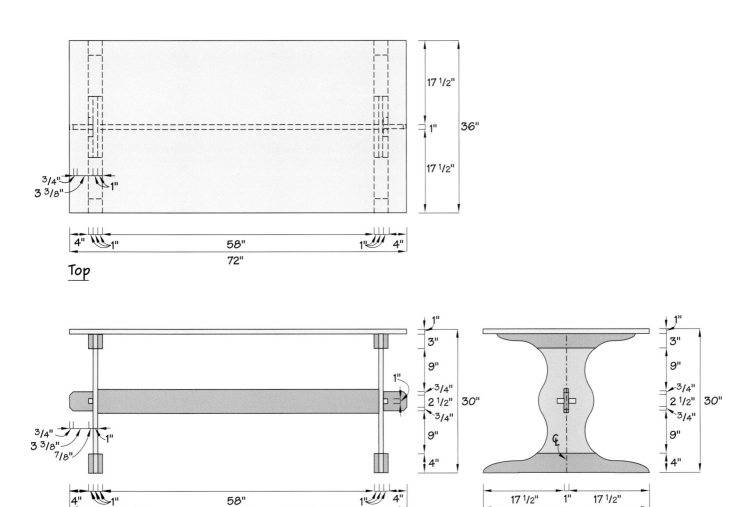

Top

17 1/2"
1"
36"
17 1/2"

3/4"
3 3/8"
1"

4" 1" 58" 1" 4"
72"

Side

1"
3 3/4"
2 1/2"
3/4"

3/4"
3 3/8"
7/8"
1"

4" 1" 58" 1" 4"
72"

1"
3"
9"
3/4"
2 1/2"
3/4"
9"
4"
30"

Front

1"
3"
9"
3/4"
2 1/2"
3/4"
9"
4"
30"

17 1/2" 1" 17 1/2"
36"

MATERIALS LIST

Trestle Table

No.	Letter	Item	Dimensions T W L
1	A	Top	1″ × 36″ × 72″
2	B	Legs	1″ × 12″ × 29″
4	C	Cleat	1″ × 4″ × 30″
4	D	Cleat	1″ × 4″ × 9″
4	E	Feet	1″ × 5″ × 36″
4	F	Feet	1″ × 5″ × 12″
1	G	Rail	1″ × 5″ × 72″
2	H	Pegs	1″ × 1½″ × 4″
8	I	Pegs	¾″dia. × 3″

SHOP TIP

Storing Biscuits

You'll keep your biscuits out of the damp, stopping them from swelling and making assembly much easier, if you keep them in an air-tight container. I use an old coffee can with a plastic lid.

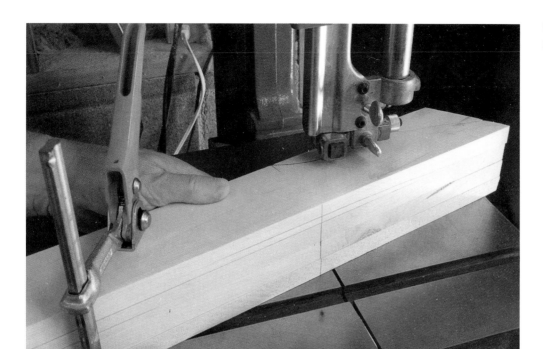

Use your band saw to cut the feet to shape.

A spindle sander makes easy work of the final shaping of the feet.

BUILDING THE TABLE

STEP 1. Cut all the pieces to size.

STEP 2. Build the board that will become the top. Alternate the growth rings to minimize the effects of warping.

STEP 3. Use a ½″ roundover bit in your router and round over the upper edge of the top.

STEP 4. Using the pattern, cut the eight shaped pieces that will form the two feet.

STEP 5. Using the pattern, cut the eight pieces that will form the two cleats.

STEP 6. Using the pattern, cut the two legs to shape.

STEP 7. Cut the mortises, one in each leg, that will accept the lower rail.

STEP 8. Cut the tenons, one on each end of the rail, as laid out in the drawing.

STEP 9. Cut the two mortises, one to each tenon, that will accept the retainer pegs.

STEP 10. Cut the two pegs to their final shape.

STEP 11. Sand all the pieces smooth and break all of the sharp edges.

STEP 12. Glue and clamp the feet and cleats (see photo) and set them aside to cure overnight.

STEP 13. Use a ³⁄₁₆″ bit in your drill press to drill pilot

Use your drill press and a ¾″ bit to mill starter holes in the legs for the mortise that will receive the rail.

Use your jigsaw to remove the rest of the waste material from the mortise.

holes in the feet and cleats to receive the screws that will fasten the understructure to the top.

STEP 14. Use a ½″ Forstner bit to countersink the pilot holes to a depth of ½″.

STEP 15. Glue and set the legs in place inside the cavities in the feet and cleats.

STEP 16. Drill ⅜″ dowel holes through the cleats and feet as laid out in the drawing.

STEP 17. Glue and set the dowels in place to strengthen the joints between the cleats, feet and legs (see photo).

STEP 18. Set the rail in place in the mortises between the two legs (see photo). Do not use glue.

STEP 19. Secure the rail in place using the two tapered pegs.

STEP 20. Set the top upside down on the bench and set the understructure in place on the underside of the top, making sure the assembly is equidistant from the ends and sides.

STEP 21. Using eight no. 10 × 3″ screws, four to each cleat and two to each side, fasten the legs to the top.

FINISHING

The best way, I think, to finish this piece is to give it a natural pine look.

First, do your finishing sanding, then some distressing—heavier around the feet and the edges of the tabletop. Next, apply an appropriate stain. I like either Bleached Mahogany by Blond-it or Puritan Pine or Golden Pecan by Minwax. To apply the stain, simply wipe it on and wipe it off; there's no need to let it stand. When the stain is dry, you can apply a little antiquing glaze. Don't overdo this; just a very light smear is enough. Finally, you can protect the piece by applying either a couple of coats of satin polyurethane or a couple of coats of Antique Oil made by Minwax.

Chapter 7

Eighteenth-Century Pembroke Table

A esthetically pleasing and a nice piece to have around the home, the Pembroke table has become something of a classic since its introduction during the second half of the eighteenth century. The first was designed by Thomas Chippendale for Lady Pembroke, hence the name. Thomas Sheraton also made a variation, but his had a serpentine top and slender, turned, reeded legs and was missing the classic lower stretchers. Ours follows Chippendale's basic design. The top is supported by square, fluted legs. On some of his designs the legs were braced by a saltire—an X-shaped stretcher—sometimes arched; ours is not.

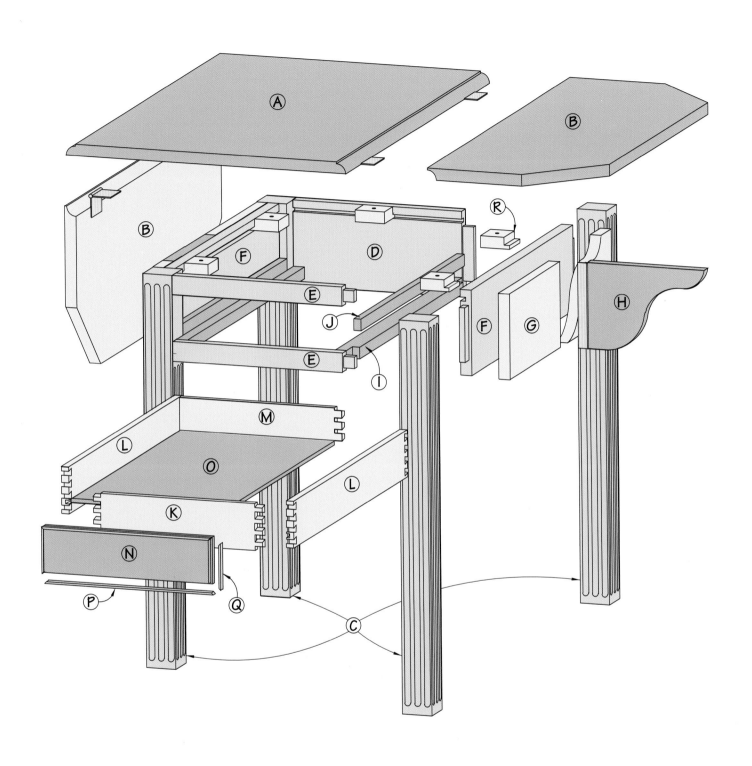

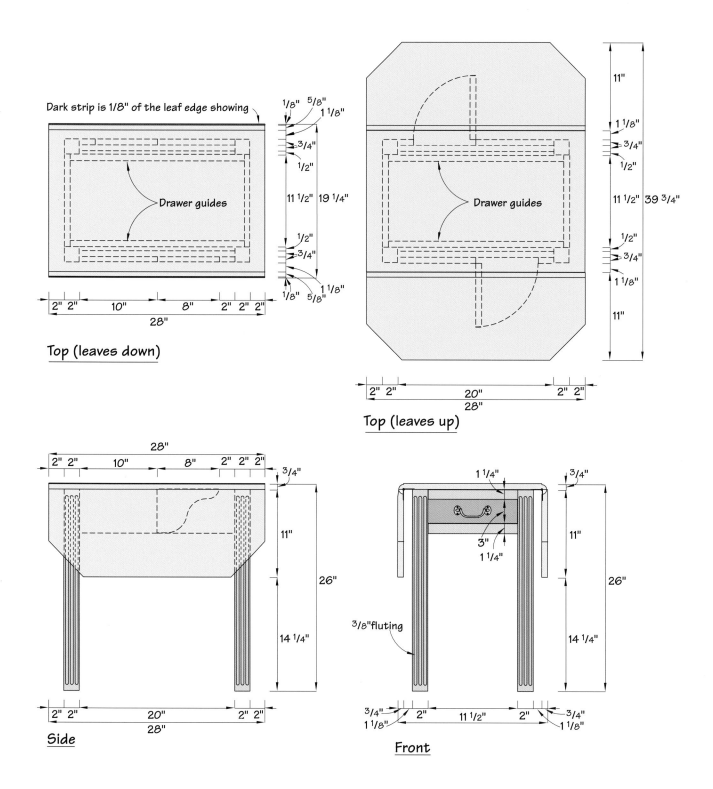

Dark strip is 1/8" of the leaf edge showing

Drawer guides

Top (leaves down)

Top (leaves up)

Side

Front

3/8"fluting

Pembroke Table Bill of Materials

No.	Letter	Item	Dimensions T W L
1	A	Top	¾″ × 19″ × 28″
2	B	Drop Leaves	¾″ × 11″ × 28″
4	C	Legs	2″ × 2″ × 4½″
1	D	*Short Apron	¾″ × 5½″ × 13″
2	E	*Rails	¾″ × 1¼″ × 13″
2	F	*Long Aprons	¾″ × 5½″ × 21½″
2	G	Fillers (long)	¾″ × 5½″ × 10″
2	H	Fillers (with wings)	¾″ × 5½″ × 10″
2	I	Drawer guides	¾″ × 1¼″ × 22½″
2	J	Drawer guides	½″ × ½″ × 20″
1	K	Drawer front	½″ × 3″ × 11½″
2	L	Sides	½″ × 3″ × 22″
1	M	Backs	½″ × 2½″ × 11½″
1	N	False Fronts	¾″ × 4¾″ × 12″
1	O	Bottoms	¼″ × 11″ × 21¾″
2	P	Beading	⅛″ × ⅜″ × 11½″
2	Q	Beading	⅛″ × ⅜″ × 3″
5	R	Top Cleats	¾″ × 2″ × 2″

*Includes Tenons

WHAT'S IT WORTH

A table like this one should sell to the trade for between $150 and $200.

CONSTRUCTION OUTLINE

Basic construction is quite simple, but a couple of features might be a little tricky. The rule joint between the top and the leaves could pose something of a challenge, and the positioning of the hinges on the underside of the top and leaves is critical (see detail on the drawing). The rule joint is cut at the router table. Two bits are used: a ½″ roundover bit for the convex cuts along the edges of the top, and a ½″ cove for the concave cuts along the edges of the leaves. Make each cut deep enough to provide a ³⁄₁₆″ shoulder. You'll need to make several passes to complete each cut, and take care to ensure the depth of the two cuts is exactly the same and that both leaves and top marry together properly (see photo). The legs are cut from a piece of 2″ × 12″ stock. The flutes are cut with a ⅜″ V-groove bit (a round nose would work just as well) in the router table. The apron and legs are joined together with mortise-and-tenon joints. Watch the positioning of the side rails; they are inset to accommodate the pad and leaf support. The front rails are made from two separate pieces of stock, mortised and tenoned to the front legs. The leaves are supported by pivoted, shaped brackets. The brackets/supports are part of a pad glued to the outer face of the two side rails. The supports themselves are attached with short sections of piano hinge, mortised into the end grain of the flap. The drawer runners and guides are glued and screwed in place. The construction of the drawer itself is quite conventional, utilizing through dovetails at the front and butt joints at the back. The drawer front has beaded edges and is glued and screwed to the front of the drawer body. The tabletop is attached to the frame with buttons. The hardware is authentic to the period. As to the finish, most Pembroke tables were made from mahogany, cherry, maple or some other hardwood, but some did have softwood tops. They were all finely finished. Ours has been stained and treated with shellac and beeswax buffed to a high shine.

BUILDING THE TABLE

STEP 1. Cut all the pieces to size, glue up the pieces for the top and make the six buttons.

STEP 2. Cut the mortises into the legs, two left and two right.

STEP 3. At the router table, cut ¼″ deep flutes into the legs—eight on each leg, two on each face—each equidistant from each edge and from each other.

STEP 4. Cut the tenons to all five pieces that make up the apron.

STEP 5. Using either your router or table saw, cut grooves to receive the buttons along the upper, inner edges of the rails that make up the apron.

STEP 6. Dry fit the apron to the legs.

STEP 7. Sand the legs and apron and set them aside for assembly later.

STEP 8. Cut the brackets from the two pieces designated for the pads and sand all of the resulting six pieces.

STEP 9. Cut the finger pulls to the curved section of each pad (see photo and drawing detail).

STEP 10. From a section of piano hinge, cut two pieces 4½′ long. You may have to drill extra screw holes.

Use your spindle sander, or a drum sander in your drill press, to cut the finger pulls in the pad and leaf support brackets. Simply hold each piece at an angle and push gently.

Try this setup for mortising the end grain of the leaf support brackets.

STEP 11. Cut mortises to receive the hinges in the ends of the brackets. Make sure you have a left- and right-hand (see the setup illustrated in photo).

STEP 12. Attach the hinges to the brackets.

STEP 13. Dry fit the pads and brackets over one of the side rails. Lay all three pieces of one set in line on top of the rail and make sure there's room enough for the bracket to pivot without fouling the outer edge of the pad. You may have to trim the end of the pad slightly and round over the inner edge of the bracket. Do the same with the second set, then set everything aside for assembly later.

STEP 14. Glue, assemble and clamp the legs and apron, and set the structure aside to cure overnight.

STEP 15. Glue and screw the pads to the outer faces of the two sides.

STEP 16. Glue and screw the drawer runners and guides to the inner face of the apron.

STEP 17. Attach the brackets to the pads. The frame is now complete.

STEP 18. Cut the angled corners to the two leaves.

STEP 19. At the router table, using a ½″ roundover bit and ½″ cover bit, cut the rule joints to the long edges of the top and the two leaves.

STEP 20. Cut the beaded edges to the front and back of the top and the outer edges of the leaves.

STEP 21. Mark out the position of the hinges to the undersides of the top and leaves. Be sure to position them exactly as laid out in the detail drawing; if you don't, the leaves will either foul the top or you'll have an unsightly gap between the two. There's no need to mortise the hinges.

STEP 22. Sand the top and leaves smooth, paying particular attention to the rules and beads. Do not assemble the top and leaves together yet.

STEP 23. Cut the through dovetails to the three pieces that make up the front of the drawer.

STEP 24. To the same three pieces, cut ¼″-wide grooves to receive the bottom, and make sure these do not foul the dovetails.

STEP 25. Assemble the drawer—butt joint the back with glue and brads.

STEP 26. Cut the beads to the edges of the drawer front.

STEP 27. Sand the drawer front smooth and then glue and screw it to the front of the drawer. Do not attach the hardware yet. You are now ready to begin the finishing process.

Use a ½″ cove bit in your router table to cut the rule joint to the inner lower edge of the leaf.

FINISHING

First you should do a little light distressing—just a small ding or two—then some final sanding before staining the pieces. I used Jacobean by Minwax. It's darker than Provincial. Now apply a sealer coat. I used shellac—seedlac at a one-pound cut left overnight to fully cure. Next, lightly sand the grain and apply four more coats of seedlac at a three-pound cut, leaving each to fully cure overnight, and rub the surface smooth—0000 steel wool is best for this and gets right into the corners of the flutes. This will give the piece a rich, dark luster. You could, of course, finish the piece with a couple of coats of polyurethane, but the look will be something less than authentic. Next, assemble the leaves to the top. Do this on the bench on a folded blanket so as not to scratch the finished surfaces. Now assemble the top to the frame. Finally, finish it all off with a couple of coats of beeswax buffed to a shine, and attach the pull to the front of the drawer.

The leaves and the tabletop should marry exactly.

Sand all the profiles smooth before staining.

Chapter 8

Library/Writing Table

These tables first appeared in America during the early 1700s. They were found most often in public places: libraries, town halls and courthouses. They were, of course, also found in many upper-class homes. The one I have chosen is an elegant piece, typical of the Queen Anne period, 1720–1750, with three drawers and turned legs. The original was a little larger. I've reduced the length from 72″ to 60″ so it will fit nicely into a smaller home.

WHAT'S IT WORTH?

In finer furniture stores you could easily pay as much as $1,600 for a reproduction table such as this.

CONSTRUCTION OUTLINE

Other than the legs (if you don't have a lathe you can use tapered legs) construction is fairly simple: the top is made from several pieces of furniture-grade pine, a full 1″ thick, biscuited and glued together; the front, back and sides are mortised and tenoned to the legs; the front is a frame made from six pieces of stock; and the legs are made from 2½″-square stock turned to an original design. The drawers have false fronts glued and screwed to through dovetail jointed carcasses. The hardware is early American and typical of the period. Finally, the piece is stained and finished with shellac to give it a deep shine.

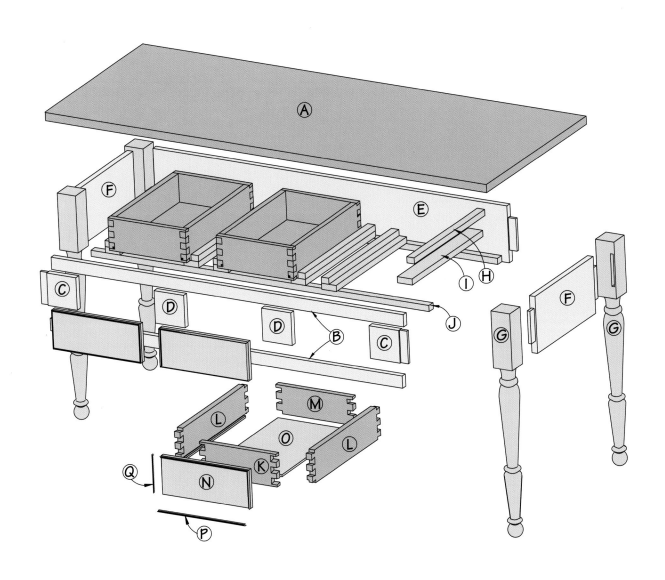

MATERIALS LIST

Library Writing Table

No.	Letter	Item	Dimensions T W L
1	A	Top	¾″ × 24″ × 60″
Apron			
2	B	*Front Apron	¾″ × 1½″ × 50″
2	C	Ends	¾″ × 4″ × 4½″
2	D	Dividers	¾″ × 4″ × 4″
1	E	*Back Apron	¾″ × 7″ × 50″
2	F	*End Aprons	¾″ × 7″ × 16″
4	G	Legs	2½″ × 2½″ × 29″
6	H	Drawer Guides	¾″ × 1″ × 16¼″
6	I	Drawer Guides	¾″ × 2″ × 16¼″
2	J	Cleats	¾″ × 1″ × 46″

No.	Letter	Item	Dimensions T W L
Drawers			
3	K	Fronts	¾″ × 4″ × 10½″
6	L	Sides	¾″ × 4″ × 16½″
3	M	Backs	¾″ × 3½″ × 10½″
3	N	False Fronts	¾″ × 4¾″ × 12″
3	O	Bottoms	¼″ × 9½″ × 16¼″
6	P	Beading	⅛″ × ⅜″ × 12″
6	Q	Beading	⅛″ × ⅜″ × 4¾″

*Includes Tenons

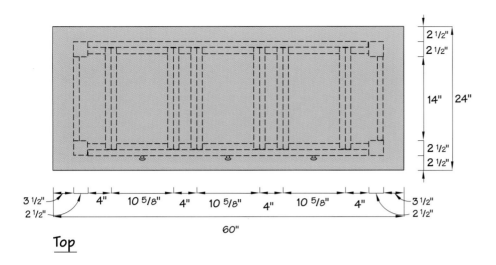

Top

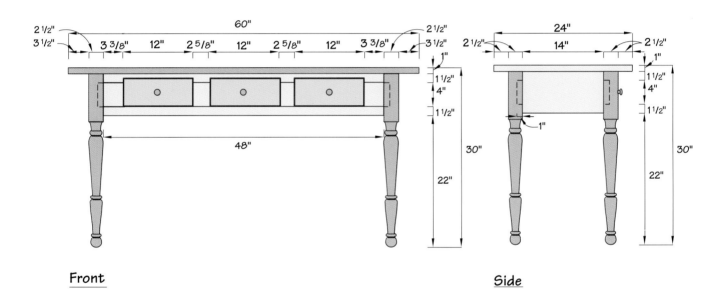

Front

Side

BUILDING THE TABLE

STEP 1. Cut all the pieces to size.

STEP 2. Build the board that will form the tabletop.

STEP 3. Use a ½″ roundover in your router and round the upper edge of the tabletop.

STEP 4. Sand the top smooth.

STEP 5. Using the scale pattern, turn the legs to shape.

STEP 6. Sand the legs smooth.

STEP 7. Cut mortises, 4″ long × ⅜″ wide × 1″ deep, to the inside faces of the tops of all four legs as laid out in the drawing.

STEP 8. Using the six pieces of stock as laid out in the drawing, build the frame that will become the front section.

STEP 9. Cut tenons, 4″ long × ⅜″ wide × 1″ deep, to the back and both sides of the apron.

STEP 10. Dry fit the apron to legs and make sure everything fits properly.

STEP 11. Disassemble the structure, then glue and clamp it and set it aside until the glue is fully cured.

STEP 12. Build the drawer guides.

STEP 13. Glue and screw the four cleats that will hold the top to the understructure in place to the top of the understructure.

STEP 14. Glue and screw the two drawer supports in

When you build the top, place your biscuits about 8″ to 10″ apart.

The front is easy to assemble. Just mark for biscuits, mill the slots, apply the glue and clamp. Leave overnight, or until the glue is fully cured, and then mill the slot for buttons that will hold the top to the subframe.

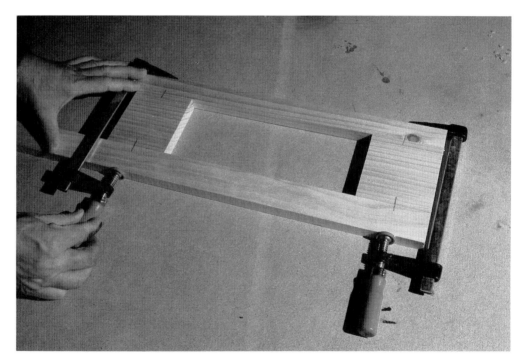

place to the lower edge of the understructure.

STEP 15. Set the drawer guides in place on the supports and secure them using no. 6 × 1¾″ screws.

STEP 16. Set the tabletop on the bench, underside up.

STEP 17. Set the carcass in place and secure to the top using ten no. 6 × 1⅝″ screws—four along each side cleat and one at each end. Elongate the holes to give the top room to breathe.

STEP 18. Using your router and dovetail jig, cut the

through dovetail joints to the fronts, sides and ends of the drawers.

STEP 19. Set your table saw to cut at a depth of ¼″ and cut the slots to the sides and fronts of the drawers that will receive the bottoms.

STEP 20. Dry fit the drawers to make sure they fit together properly, then glue, clamp and square them, and leave them overnight or until the glue has fully cured.

STEP 21. Use your router and a ¼″ roundover bit to trim

When you've milled the slot in the rails for the buttons that will hold the top to the sub-frame, you can use your trusty tenoning jig to cut the tenons.

The drawer guides are easily made from two pieces of stock, glued and clamped together. If you like, you can secure them with a couple of screws for extra strength.

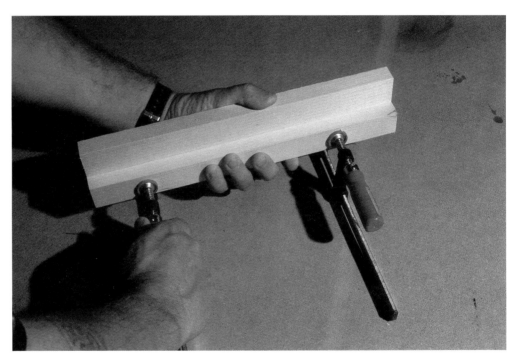

the edges of the false drawer fronts to their final shape.

STEP 22. Complete the construction of the drawers by fastening the hardware to the false fronts, the false fronts to the carcasses and the bottoms to the slots provided.

STEP 23. Do the final finish sanding. You'll need to take your time over this stage. The better the job you do, the better the final finish will be.

FINISHING

I wanted a light finish for this piece, so I chose Puritan Pine stain made by Minwax. This I topped off with four coats of orange shellac at a three-pound cut. Each coat was allowed to dry for twenty-four hours before the next was applied. Also, I lightly sanded between coats with 400-grit paper.

Chapter 9

Eighteenth-Century Dower Chest

For hundreds of years, at least from the time of the Norman Conquest in England, chests like this were traditionally built for a girl when she reached ten years of age. In it she would store personal items, her own needlework and other bits and pieces accumulated over the years preceding her marriage. Today the tradition is still alive, but now the dower is called a hope chest. During medieval times the chest was a very heavy piece, constructed usually from oak. Later they were made mostly of pine. Few have survived the

centuries. Those that have are all in museums. During Elizabethan times the chests were still heavy but more intricate in design, usually featuring panel construction. Early American versions were often simple six-board affairs. Later they were much better made with dovetail joints and one or two drawers below the chest. Some had tills (small trays) just inside the top. Most, especially Pennsylvania German versions, were hand painted with lots of color and, perhaps, flowers or animals. The dower chest was usually painted a soft blue

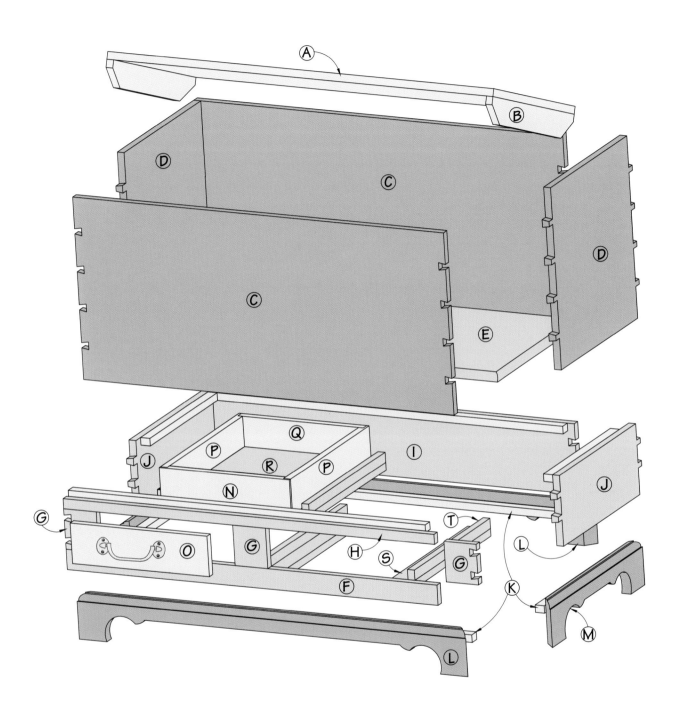

color. Unfortunately, examples with the original paint are extremely rare. The one I have chosen is a copy of a dower chest made in Bucks County, Pennsylvania, circa 1780. The original was hand painted with a variety of designs. Not being much of an artist, I left out the designs, preferring instead a heavily aged, distressed look.

WHAT'S IT WORTH?

The cost in materials for this piece should run between $40 and $60, including hardware and paint. You'll put at least twenty hours into it. I have sold a number of these chests to the trade at $295; they retail around $500 more or less, depending upon the type of outlet.

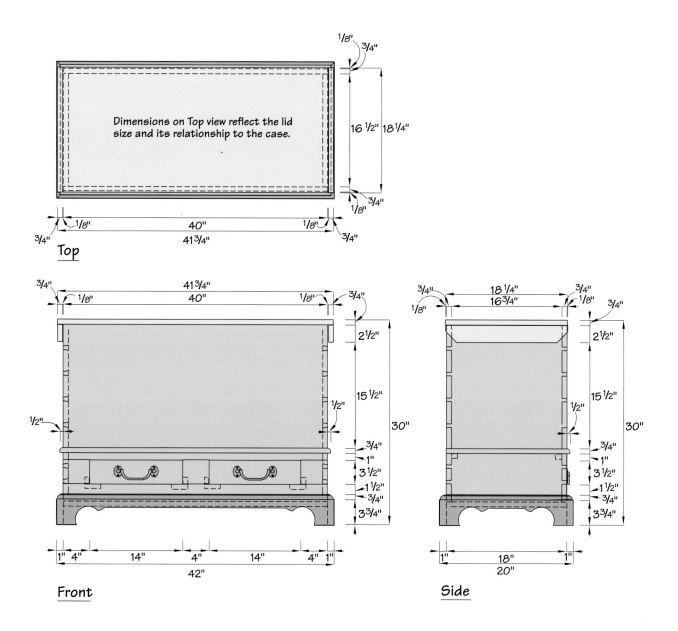

Dimensions on Top view reflect the lid size and its relationship to the case.

Top

Front

Side

CONSTRUCTION OUTLINE

Construction of this piece is quite challenging. Both sections of the chest are constructed using dovetail joints. Whether you put the tails on the ends or the sides is a matter of aesthetics and personal choice. I quite like the large end grains showing, so I put mine on the face of the piece; you should do whatever pleases you most.

The front of the lower section containing the drawers is made from five pieces of stock. Inside, the drawer runners and guides are secured to cleats that run the entire length of the front and back. The drawers themselves are constructed using simple lap joints, as was the case for many of the earliest versions. You can use half-blind dovetails if you prefer. The top and bottom,

sides and ends of the upper section are constructed from two, three or four pieces of stock; the end grains are alternated for stability. Cleats are fastened to the undersides of both ends of the top, again for stability. These are held in place with glue and biscuits; dowels would do just as well. The lower skirt, which includes the feet, is mitered to fit around the lower section, then screwed in place from the inside; only the miters are glued. Hardware for a piece such as this is always a problem. I used drawer pulls salvaged from an old piece. The "H" hinges are reproductions. You could use piano hinges but, as always, that would not look right. You'll also need to insert a lid support of some sort.

Dower Chest

No.	Letter	Item	Dimensions T W L
Top			
1	A	Top	¾″ × 41¾″ × 18¼″
2	B	Cleats	¾″ × 2¼″ × 18¼″
Upper Chest			
2	C	Front and Back	¾″ × 40″ × 18″
2	D	Ends	¾″ × 18″ × 18″
1	E	Bottom	¾″ × 41″ × 18½″
Drawer Section			
1	F	Front Lower Rail	¾″ × 2″ × 40″
2	G	Front Stiles	¾″ × 4″ × 3½″
1	H	Front Upper Rail	¾″ × 1″ × 40″
1	I	Back	¾″ × 6″ × 40″
2	J	Ends	¾″ × 6″ × 18″
4	K	Cleats	¾″ × 1″ × 38½″
*2	L	Front and Rear Feet	¾″ × 4½″ × 42½″
*2	M	End Feet	¾″ × 4½″ × 20½″
Drawers			
2	N	Fronts	¾″ × 3½″ × 14″
2	O	False Fronts	¾″ × 4½″ × 15″
4	P	Sides	¾″ × 3½″ × 17″
2	Q	Backs	¾″ × 3″ × 13″
2	R	Bottoms	¾″ × 17″ × 13″
4	S	Guides	¾″ × 2½″ × 17″
4	T	Guides	¾″ × 1″ × 17″

*Leave extra length for cutting miters

BUILDING THE CHEST

STEP 1. Cut all the parts to size.

STEP 2. Build the boards that will make up the front, back, ends, bottom and lid of the upper chest.

STEP 3. Build the front of the lower section. You can use biscuits, dowels or simple butt joints to secure the five pieces. Glue, clamp and set aside to cure overnight.

STEP 4. Sand the front of the lower section smooth.

STEP 5. If you have a dovetail jig—I use Leigh's—turn the guide fingers to the TD mode and set the fingers at roughly 2½″ intervals (see photo). This will work quite nicely for both upper and lower sections.

STEP 6. Turn the guide fingers over and cut the tails to the front and rear boards of the upper chest and the front and rear of the lower section.

STEP 7. Turn the guide fingers back to the TD mode, set the assembly to cut the pins slightly oversize (see Shop Tip) and cut the pins to the edge of one of the ends of the upper chest.

STEP 8. Remove the work piece from the jig and test the fit to either the front or back of the upper chest. The fit should be tight. If the pins are too large, reset the jig, replace the workpiece in the jig and recut the pins. *Be sure you don't cut them too small* (see Shop Tip).

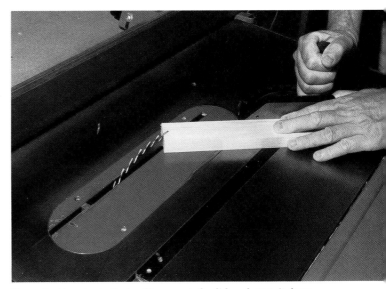

To make the cleats that will support the lid and stop it from warping, cut your stock to size, and then cut the corners away at a 90° angle.

Fasten the cleats to the lid with biscuits and glue, and then clamp the assembly and leave it overnight, or until the glue is fully cured.

When forming the feet, it's a good idea to cut the miters before you cut the details.

STEP 9. When you've recut the pins, test the fit once again. If you have it right, continue on and cut the pins to the remaining pieces of the upper and lower sections.

STEP 10. Use plenty of glue to assemble the dovetailed sections; I use one of the new polyurethane glues. Glue, assemble and clamp both the upper and lower sections. Check both to make sure they are perfectly square. Set both sections aside to cure overnight.

STEP 11. Using a ½″ bit in your router, round over the two ends and front edge of the bottom.

STEP 12. Turn the upper section of the chest so the bottom is uppermost and place it on the bench. Set the bottom board in place, making sure it is flush with rear of the chest and projects at the front and equally at both ends. Now, using ten no. $6 \times 1\frac{3}{4}″$ screws—four along each side and one at each end—fasten the bottom board to the chest walls.

STEP 13. Using glue and screws, assemble the two long cleats that will support the drawer guides to the lower section as laid out in the drawing.

STEP 14. Using glue and screws, assemble the two long cleats that will secure the lower section to the upper chest as laid out in the drawing.

STEP 15. Build the four drawer guides as laid out in the drawing.

STEP 16. Using glue and screws, assemble and fasten the

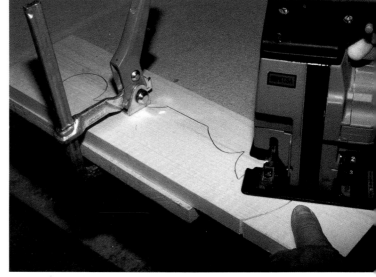

Your jigsaw is the best tool for cutting out the detail to the feet.

drawer guides to the lower set of cleats on the lower section. Be sure they run square to the openings.

STEP 17. With the chest still bottom up on the bench, place the lower section upside down on the underside of the upper chest and set it in place so both upper and lower sections align perfectly.

STEP 18. Using ten no. $6 \times 1\frac{3}{4}″$ screws—four along each side and one at each end—fasten the lower section to the upper chest.

STEP 19. Using the pattern, cut the detail to all four sections of the feet.

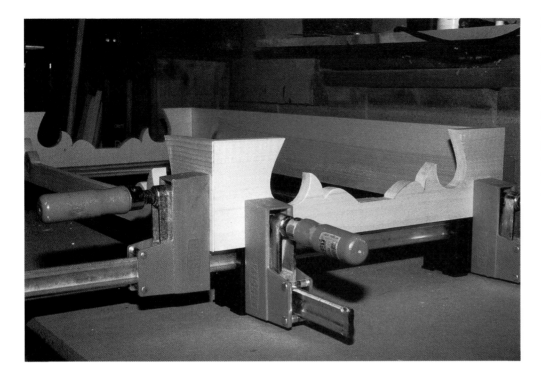

Bessy's system of blocks and clamps makes the assembly of the mitered feet section a simple job. Set the clamps in the block, glue the miters, assemble the pieces, apply slight pressure with the clamps, make sure all is square, and then fully tighten the clamps and leave the piece overnight, or until the glue has fully cured.

STEP 20. Cut the feet sections accurately to length and miter the ends to 45°.

STEP 21. Cut the cleats to length and glue and screw them in place, 1″ from the top, on the inside of the feet sections as you see in the drawing.

STEP 22. Still with the chest assembly upside down on the bench, from the inside of the lower section, screw the front and rear feet sections in place.

STEP 23. From the inside, and using a little glue on the miters, screw the two end-feet sections in place. Set the assembly aside and leave overnight or until the glue fully cures.

STEP 24. Using a ½″ bit in your router, round over the top edge of two ends and both edges of the top front.

STEP 25. Mark the cleats and lid for biscuit slots.

STEP 26. Mill the biscuit slots to the cleats and lid.

STEP 27. Glue and clamp the cleats to the lid, set aside and leave overnight to cure.

STEP 28. Finish sand the entire assembly using 220-grit paper, *but do not assemble the lid to the chest yet.* Wait until the finishing is complete.

STEP 29. Using simple lap joints, build the drawers as you see in the drawing.

STEP 30. Using a ¼″ bit in your router, round over the edges of the two drawer false fronts.

STEP 31. Fasten the drawer pulls to the false fronts.

STEP 32. Using four no. 6 × 1¼″ screws—two to each drawer—fasten the false fronts to the drawers.

STEP 33. Assemble and fasten the drawer bottoms.

STEP 34. Apply the finish to all sections (see page 62).

STEP 35. Using three hinges, assemble the lid to the chest.

STEP 36. Assemble the lid support to the inside of the chest and lid.

SHOP TIP
Leigh Dovetail Jig

To ensure optimum results from your Leigh dovetail jig, or any dovetail jig, make sure the workpiece touches not only the two stops on lower left of the jig *but the underside of all of the fingers.* Failure to do this will cause a slight misalignment—steps at the bottom and top edges—between the sections.

FINISHING

I chose an old painted look for this piece. You can follow my lead or simply stain it and give it a couple of coats of polyurethane, but that would miss the point somewhat.

The peeling painted finish you see in the color shot will take a bit of work, but the final effect is well worth the effort and you'll end up with a chest that does, indeed, look a couple of hundred years old. It's very effective and simple to achieve.

STEP 1. First you'll need to do some distressing. Over an extended number of years, a piece like this would receive quite a beating. The upper edges of the chest would have been extensively knocked about, as would the corners of both sections and feet. The top front to edge of the chest would have been heavily worn and rounded. The corners would have rounded over. The lid would have a lot of dents and dings, and I wore away the front edge and inward from the edge for about six inches to duplicate the wear one might expect from a couple of hundred years of people sitting on it. You really can't go overboard on a piece like this.

STEP 2. Next, apply an appropriate stain to give the wood an underlying patina. I chose Minwax's Provincial, but Early American or Blond-it's Bleached Mahogany would have done just as well.

STEP 3. To achieve the peeling paint look you see in the photo, follow the steps for the Peeling Paint Effect on page 22 of chapter three.

STEP 4. Now you'll need to apply the wear and tear of

see the steps for the Peeling Paint Effect on page 22 of chapter three.

SHOP TIP
Cutting Tight Dovetails

It may cause something of a struggle during assembly, but I recommend you set your dovetail jig to cut the tails a little tighter than for a normal fit. The tendency for long sections of joints such as this is to cut them slack to make assembly easier.

Unfortunately, this will have several effects. First the joint will be weak and subsequently the glue may break. Second, you'll have a lot of filling to do between the pins and tails. Finally, you'll have to clamp almost every pin and tail to bring everything together while the glue cures. Cut the tails for a tight fit and you'll not only eliminate all of the above, but the pins will pull the joint tightly together and the resulting assembly will be almost perfectly square.

the ages. Using 320-grit wet-and-dry and a lot of water, wear away the paint to the polyurethane coats below but take care not to go too deep. Show the bare, unstained wood and you'll spoil the entire finish. Also, be careful to use only the lightest pressure for the rubbing down; the paint may still tend to strip.

STEP 5. Finally, apply a light film of antiquing glaze—don't overdo this—and seal the finish with a couple of coats of satin polyurethane.

Assemble the lid to the chest and you're done.

Chapter 10

Nineteenth-Century Dry Sink

These pieces first came into use in the mid-eighteenth century. They were simple pieces found in the kitchens of country homes throughout America. They were used to hold water; a basin was simply placed in the well. Most incorporated a cupboard below and some even had drawers where towels and pots and pans and dishes were stored. Most of the early pieces were made from pine, but oak, poplar and maple

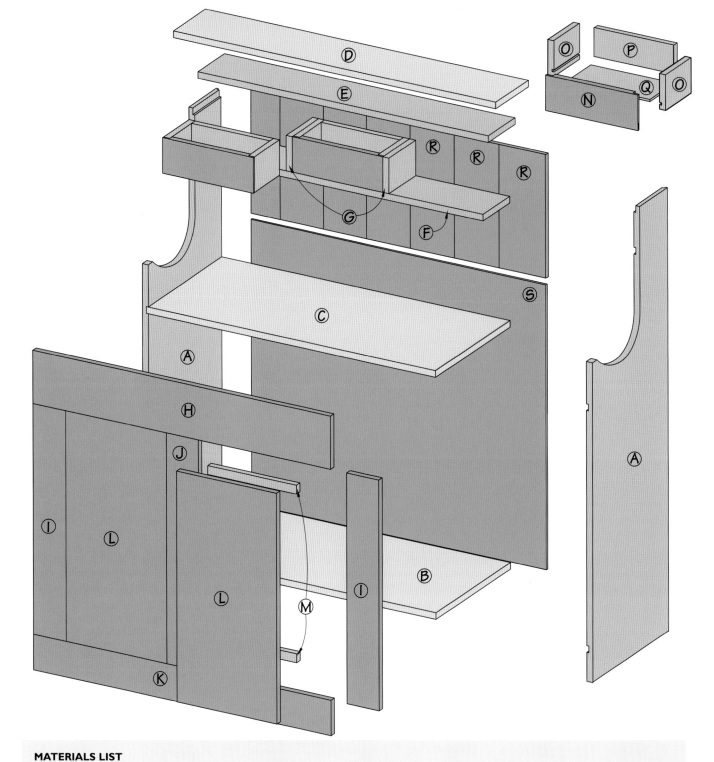

MATERIALS LIST

Low Dry Sink

No.	Letter	Item	Dimensions T W L
Material			
2	A	Stiles	¾″ × 2½″ × 29¾″
1	B	Center Stile	¾″ × 3″ × 31½″
1	C	Rail	¾″ × 2½″ × 36½″
2	D	Doors	¾″ × 14¼″ × 29½″
2	E	Ends	¾″ × 15¾″ × 34″
3	F	Shelves	¾″ × 15½″ × 35½″
1	G	Top	¾″ × 18″ × 38″

No.	Letter	Item	Dimensions T W L
2	H	Sink Ends	¾″ × 4½″ × 18″
1	I	Sink Front	¾″ × 5″ × 38″
1	J	Sink Back	¾″ × 4½″ × 36½″
1	K	Sink Top	¾″ × 4½″ × 38″
3	L	End Base	¾″ × 3½″ × 18″
3	M	Front and Back Base	¾″ × 3½″ × 36″
3	N	Back	¼″ × 36″ × 34″

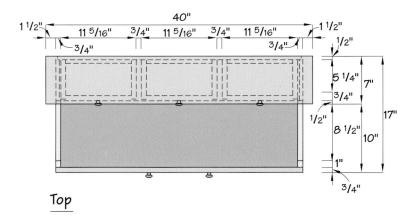

Top

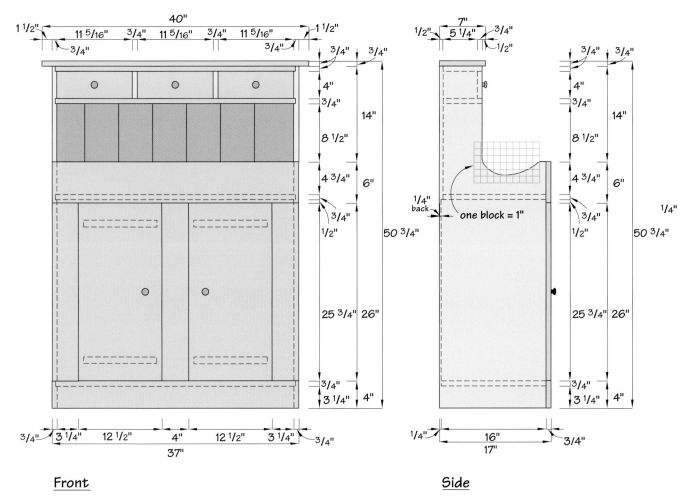

Front

one block = 1"

Side

were also used. Most were painted in dark colors—green, black or brown. Many were left unfinished, scrubbed and rescrubbed over the years. Today, they are enjoying a new popularity due very much to the country crafting community.

The dry sink I've chosen for this book is an attractive piece, simple in design and easy enough to make over a weekend. The period? I'm not sure. I found the original, an authentic antique, illustrated in a book on antique American furniture. It wasn't dated, but I estimate

it must have been made during the early part of the nineteenth century.

WHAT'S IT WORTH?

You'll find craft-made dry sinks for sale in one form or another at outdoor craft fairs, craft shops and the like all across the country, and at prices that reflect the quality: from $120 to $350. They are, after all, simple pieces.

CONSTRUCTION OUTLINE

The carcass is a simple structure. The sides are made all in one piece and shaped to form the top section. They are rabbeted and dadoed to accept a single shelf that forms the cupboard bottom, the bottom of the sink area, the support for the drawers above the sink and a false top to which the top itself is fastened with screws. There are no inner shelves to allow for storage of large items such as buckets, churns and other containers. The doors are simple flat panels, and the drawers are constructed using simple lap joints. The back of the upper section is made from pieces of ½"-thick stock, edged on one side and butted together—no tongue-and-groove joints; the lower back is made from a single piece of ¼" lauan plywood. You could use lauan plywood for all of the back, but that would destroy the antique look of the piece. A dedicated weekend of work should see the piece ready for finishing. As to finishing, the original piece was extremely attractive—that's why I chose it—and I saw no reason to change the look.

BUILDING THE DRY SINK

STEP 1. Cut all the pieces to size.

STEP 2. Build the two boards that will form the sides.

STEP 3. Build the two boards that will form the bottom of the cupboard and the bottom of the sink area.

STEP 4. Build the two boards that will form the doors.

STEP 5. Cut the sides to shape as per the drawing. It's best to use a handheld jigsaw for this process.

When you mill the dado to the sides, you can use either your radial arm saw or a router with a ¾" bit. If you use both the router and the T square, you'll find it easier to make matching cuts if you clamp both sides together and run the router over both pieces.

STEP 6. Sand all the pieces smooth.

STEP 7. Mill the dadoes in the sides as per the drawing. Make sure you have a left and a right.

STEP 8. Glue, toenail and clamp the cupboard bottom, sink bottom, drawer support and false top to the dadoes and rabbet in the sides, and set the structure aside until the glue is fully cured.

STEP 9. There are several ways to attach the trim to the carcass. You can glue, nail and clamp as I did, and as was done on the original, or you can biscuit them on. I believe, because the original was a simple country structure, the way to go is to use nails and fill the holes. They'll still show, but that's good and adds to the overall look of the piece.

STEP 10. Glue, nail and clamp the front of the sink area to the carcass.

STEP 11. Glue, nail and clamp the side trim and the center trim to the carcass.

STEP 12. Toenail the side trim and the center trim to the front of the sink area.

STEP 13. Set the nail heads and fill the holes with wood putty.

STEP 14. Set the top in place on the false top and, from underneath, fasten the two together with no. 6 × 1⅝" screws.

STEP 15. Use glue and screws to fasten the drawer dividers in place; plug the screw holes.

STEP 16. Use ¾" stock 4½" × 18"—or assorted widths for a pleasing effect—and no. 6 × 1½" screws, and form the ends of the sink top.

STEP 17. Fit the doors to the carcass. Trim for a good fit as necessary.

STEP 18. Cut mortises in the edges of the doors and frames to receive brass butt hinges. Do not attach the doors yet.

STEP 19. Cut and sand the two swivel catches as you see in the drawing.

STEP 20. Build the three small drawers using simple lap joints and cut-steel nails.

STEP 21. For a really authentic look, resaw some narrow stock to make ¼" boards to form the bottoms of the drawers.

To prevent the doors from warping, screw and glue cleats across the widths of the backs. For doors this size, you'll need three cleats, one at each end and one in the middle.

STEP 22. Do any necessary finish sanding and break all the sharp edges.

STEP 23. Go to the finishing process below.

STEP 24. Attach the doors to the carcass.

STEP 25. Attach the lower back to the carcass using 1″ brads.

STEP 26. Attach the hardware to the doors and drawers.

STEP 27. Set the swivel catches in place and fasten with no. $6 \times 1\frac{5}{8}″$ screws.

FINISHING

No secrets here other than the stain. I chose tobacco juice and then finished it with a couple of coats of satin polyurethane for protection.

As always, you'll find your tenoning jig is the best tool for forming the rabbets to the drawer fronts.

Chapter 11

Late Eighteenth-Century Welsh Dresser

The Welsh dresser is something of an enigma. There seems to be little restriction as to size and form of this traditional piece. I've seen huge examples. One, I recall, in the Childswickham Arms, one of the oldest pubs in England, is some eight feet wide and seven feet tall, with shelves stacked with antique pewter plates, pots and jugs. Another, imported into the United States from England, for sale in an antique

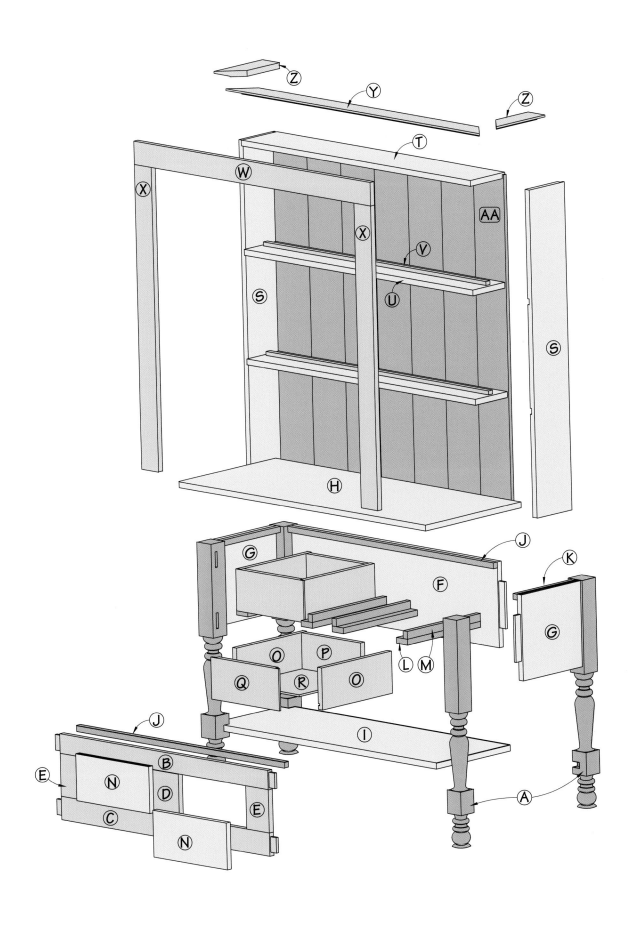

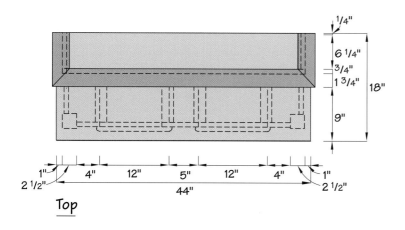

Top

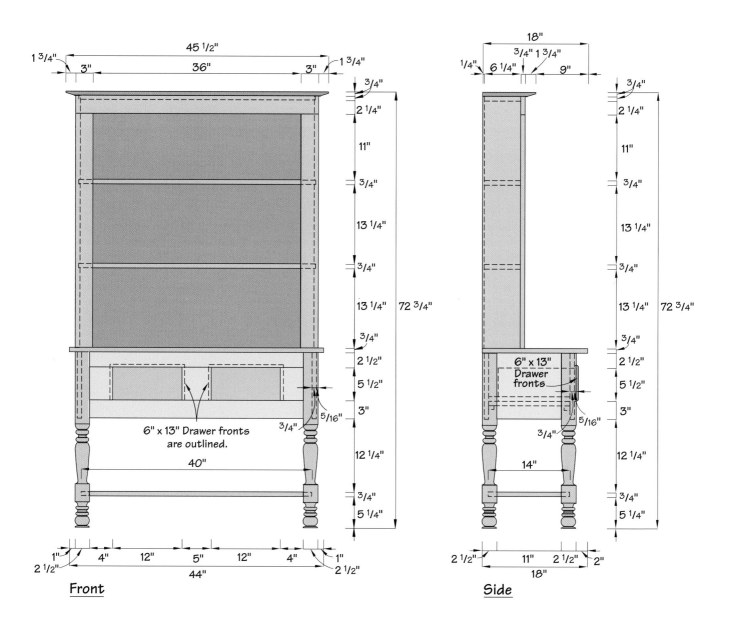

6" x 13" Drawer fronts
are outlined.

Front

6" x 13"
Drawer
fronts

Side

Welsh Dresser

No.	Letter	Item	Dimensions T W L
4	A	Legs	2 ½″ × 2½″ × 29¼″
1	B	*Front	¾″ × 2½″ × 39″
1	C	*Front	¾″ × 3″ × 39″
1	D	Front	¾″ × 5½″ × 5″
2	E	Fronts	¾″ × 5½″ × 4″
1	F	*Lower Back	¾″ × 11″ × 39″
2	G	Lower Sides	¾″ × 11″ × 13″
1	H	Work Top	¾″ × 18″ × 48″
1	I	**Shelf	¾″ × 14″ × 40″
4	J	Cleats	¾″ × 1″ × 37″
2	K	Cleats	¾″ × 1″ × 10¾″
4	L	Drawer Guides	¾″ × 2″ × 13⅞″
4	M	Drawer Guides	¾″ × 1″ × 13⅞″
2	N	Drawer False Front	¾″ × 6″ × 13″
4	O	Drawer Sides	¾″ × 5⅜″ × 13″
2	P	Drawer Backs	¾″ × 4⅞″ × 10½″
2	Q	Drawer Fronts	¾″ × 5⅜″ × 12″
2	R	Drawer Bottoms	¾″ × 11″ × 12½″
2	S	Upper Sides	¾″ × 6½″ × 42″
2	T	Upper Top	¾″ × 6½″ × 41″
3	U	Upper Shelves	¾″ × 6″ × 41″
2	V	Plate Strips	½″ × ¾″ × 40″
1	W	Trim	¾″ × 3″ × 42″
2	X	Trim	¾″ × 3″ × 39″
1	Y	Crown	¾″ × 3″ × 45½″
2	Z	Crown	¾″ × 3″ × 9″
6	AA	Back	½″ × 7⅛″ × 41½″

*Includes Tenons
**Cutting allowance included

dealer's store in Atlanta was even bigger, at least ten feet wide. Then again, I've seen small versions not more than 30″ wide and 66″ tall. The design, and there are two primary versions, takes its name from Wales, a small part of the United Kingdom, where it's supposed to have originated. The earliest versions, made prior to and including the early eighteenth century, were rather crude affairs made primarily by village carpenters. By the turn of the nineteenth century, however, the piece had evolved to the point where it could be regarded as fine furniture, suitable to grace even the finest of drawing rooms. Even so, the basic design remained true to the original traditional form and still does today.

As previously mentioned, there are two basic forms of Welsh dresser: One has a cupboard-bottom and an open-shelf upper dresser; the other, the one we shall be dealing with, is called a "pot-board" Welsh dresser. The original was made in the late 1700s. It has the usual open-shelf upper dresser, but the lower section has two deep drawers side by side and is supported by turned legs connected by a low shelf. This I believe to be the more traditional of the two styles. And, most important, at least to me, it's certainly the more aesthetically appealing of the two designs. It's a challenging piece to build, will take many hours and will involve the use of every tool in the shop. When it's finished you'll have a family heirloom you can be justly proud of; I certainly am of mine.

WHAT'S IT WORTH?

This, of course, depends on how good a job you've made of it. But let's assume you've made a nice piece. You should be able to sell it for at least $1,400, perhaps as much as $1,800. An eighteenth-century original would fetch at least $6,000 and possibly as much as $10,000.

CONSTRUCTION OUTLINE

Construction is quite straightforward, but there are a couple of tricky areas you should be aware of: the attachment of the lower shelf to the legs and the legs themselves. The legs are made from 2½″ furniture-grade stock, cut to size, planed smooth and then turned on the lathe to an authentic eighteenth-century pattern. Pine is not the best material for turning, but with time and care you should be able to do a good job. The lower shelf is attached by way of two-way mortises cut into the corners of the legs. To do this I used a combination of dovetail saw and dedicated mortising machine. If you don't have the machine, it would be quite easy to do with a saw and a good sharp chisel.

The upper section is constructed using simple dadoes to attach the shelves to the sides. The back is made from boards of irregular widths, just as was the original, and is fastened to the lower section with removable screws so the piece can be taken down for transportation.

The lower section is constructed using traditional mortise-and-tenon joints to secure the front, back and sides to the legs. The front is made from five separate pieces of stock. The top is made from two pieces of furniture-grade stock a full 1″ thick after planing and sanding. The drawers are constructed using lap joints and cut-steel nails, as were those in the original. You can use dovetails if you desire.

For the finish, I chose painted crackle green over red to match the pie safe described in chapter sixteen. Since then, I've made a second piece and finished it using a dark stain and eight coats of orange shellac followed by a couple of applications of beeswax. Either way, it's a stunning piece.

It will take at least forty hours to construct and finish this traditional Welsh dresser, but the result will please you beyond your expectations.

BUILDING THE DRESSER

STEP 1. Cut all the pieces to size.

STEP 2. Build the boards that will become the shelf and top of the lower section. You can do this using your plate jointer and biscuits or dowels. The dimensions given for the lower shelf are slightly larger than the finished piece. This allows you to cut it to the exact size once the lower section can be dry fitted together.

STEP 3. Using five pieces of stock, build the front of the lower section as laid out in the drawing. Be sure to make the offsets to incorporate the tenons.

STEP 4. Using the scale pattern, turn the legs. Take care to remove material in very small bites using very sharp tools, and take time to do a good job of the sanding. Even the smallest ring will show dark when you apply the stain. I suggest you do the first finishing steps to the legs before going any further—at least to the sealing and sanding stage—as you'll find in the Shop Tip on page 75.

STEP 5. Cut dadoes and rabbets ¼″ deep to the sides of the upper section as laid out in the drawing.

STEP 6. Glue, clamp and toenail the shelves and top to the sides of the upper section. Check the structure is square, then set it aside to fully cure.

STEP 7. Using either your dedicated mortising machine, mortising attachment in your drill press or hammer and chisel, cut ⅜″ mortises, 6″ long and 1″ deep, into the inner faces of the rear legs to accept the tenons you'll cut to the back and both sides.

STEP 8. Cut two mortises to the front inner faces of the two front legs, ⅜″ wide, 2″ long and 1″ deep, to accept

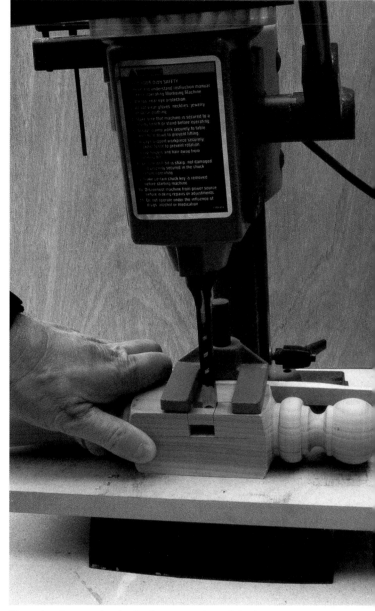

To make the mortise in the lower section of the legs, you can begin by using either your dedicated mortising machine, mortising attachment for your drill press or those good old hand tools. Mark out the position of the mortise, making sure you have a left and right, and front and back, and then remove the waste, first from one side and then the other.

the tenons of the front section as laid out in the drawing, and a single mortise to each inner side face of each front leg to accept the sides. These should be ⅜″ wide, 6″ long and 1″ deep.

STEP 9. Cut the two-way mortises you see in the drawing and photo above to accept the lower shelf.

STEP 10. Cut the tenons to the back, sides and front of the lower section.

STEP 11. Dry assemble the lower section to ensure a good fit and clamp it to ensure everything is tightly together.

STEP 12. Measure the distance between the backs of the mortises that will accept the lower shelf. Measure from side to side and from back to front. Ensure you do this accurately; the final fit and appearance will depend on how well you do this.

STEP 13. Disassemble the structure.

STEP 14. Cut the lower shelf accurately to size.

STEP 15. Assemble the lower section in the following *specific* order.

STEP 16. Using one of the new polyurethane products, glue and clamp the back to the two rear legs and set the result aside until the glue is fully cured, at least twelve hours.

STEP 17. Do the same for the two front legs and the front section.

STEP 18. When the glue is fully cured, remove the clamps from the back and front sections and set the back section on the bench with the mortises that will accept the sides facing up.

STEP 19. Glue the two sides in place.

STEP 20. Apply glue to the two-way mortises that will accept the lower shelf, then set the shelf in place.

STEP 21. Take the front leg section, apply glue to all of the mortises and the tenons of the two sides.

STEP 22. Set the front leg section in place on the tenons and the lower shelf.

STEP 23. Stand the structure on its feet on a flat surface and clamp everything in place.

STEP 24. Check to make sure everything is square and the piece stands squarely on its feet. If you need to make adjustments, do so by adjusting the alignment of the clamps.

STEP 25. When all is satisfactory, set the structure aside for at least twelve hours to ensure the glue cures completely.

STEP 26. Remove the clamps and, using glue and screws, attach the cleats that will secure the top to the inside of the lower section.

STEP 27. Glue and screw the cleats that will support the drawer guides in place, as laid out in the drawing.

STEP 28. Build the drawer guides and, using glue and screws, fasten them in place on their support. Make sure they are square to the front.

STEP 29. Now, using twelve no. $8 \times 1\frac{5}{8}''$ screws, five along front and back and one at each end, fasten the top to the cleats. Be sure to elongate the holes slightly to allow room for the top to breathe.

STEP 30. Returning to the upper section, slightly round over the edges of the boards that make up the back.

Now you can use either your table saw or hand saw to remove the small strip that remains.

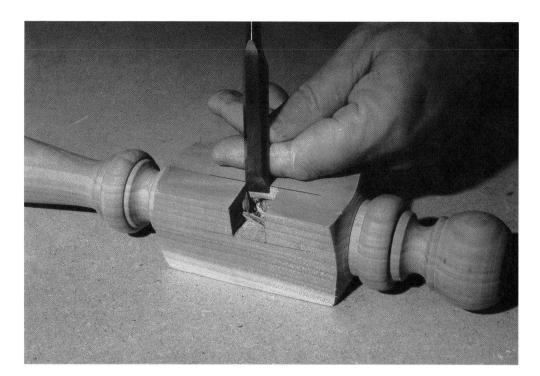

Clean out the mortise with a chisel, but be careful not to remove too much material or the joint will be sloppy.

Finally, dry fit the shelf to the leg. If all is well, the joint should be nice and tight. When you complete the final assembly, you can use a small amount of glue inside the mortise.

STEP 31. Screw the back boards in place, roundovers facing forward. If you've used odd widths, you can set them in place with widest in the center or in no particular order as I did. The result is pleasing whichever way you do it.

STEP 32. Set your table saw to cut at an angle of 17°. You will use this to mill the bevels to the three pieces that make up the crown.

STEP 33. Mill the bevel to the three pieces that will make up the crown as laid out in the drawing. It's best you do this using a single piece of stock, then cut the three pieces from it when the detail is complete.

STEP 34. Glue and screw the crown in place on top of the upper section.

STEP 35. Tack and glue the plate-stop strips to the shelves as laid out in the drawing.

STEP 36. Set the top section in place on the lower section, make sure it stands square, then drill four screw holes through the lower edge of the back. These will take the screws that will hold the upper and lower sections together. Don't fasten them together yet.

STEP 37. If the upper section is square to the lower section, remove it and set it aside. If not, make any necessary adjustments and try again.

STEP 38. Build the drawers as per the drawing and the Shop Tip on page 98.

You can use your tenoning jig to cut the tenons to the ends of the front, as well as the back and sides of the lower case, just as you would with any solid piece of stock.

Attach the trim to the front of the upper case with biscuits and glue. Mark the sides and edge of the trim, and cut the slots in both. Just remember that the mark will always point toward the machine.

FINISHING

You have a choice here. As mentioned earlier, I finished the one you see in the color photo to match the pie safe in chapter sixteen. If you decide to do the same, find the technique described there and in chapter three.

If you decide to go with stain and shellac, you'll find that technique described in chapter three. Whichever you choose, take your time and do a good job, especially where the legs are concerned. The turnings are difficult to do and will take a lot of care and attention.

SHOP TIP
Sanding and Finishing a Turned Leg or Spindle

Turned legs, once they are assembled to the rest of the piece, can be a real pain to sand smooth, especially if you've used a water-based product that raises the grain. You can make life a lot simpler if you do the following. Once you've sanded the leg smooth, remove it from the lathe and do any necessary staining, sealing, polyurethane coating, etc. When all the coats have dried completely, return the leg to the lathe, set the machine to its slowest speed and start it turning. Then, using either 320- or 400-grit sandpaper, lightly sand the turned sections until they are nice and smooth. Finally, remove the leg from the lathe and apply a final coat of finish.

Chapter 12

Colonial Washstand Circa 1760

I found the original of this piece while on vacation on Jekyll Island in Georgia. It was one of a pair in a conference room at the Jekyll Island Club Hotel, part of the island's historic district, and was probably made during the middle of the eighteenth century. It was, as ours is, made from pine. The patina was a lovely buttery color. Close inspection failed to reveal traces of any finish other than many years of wax polishing. Most

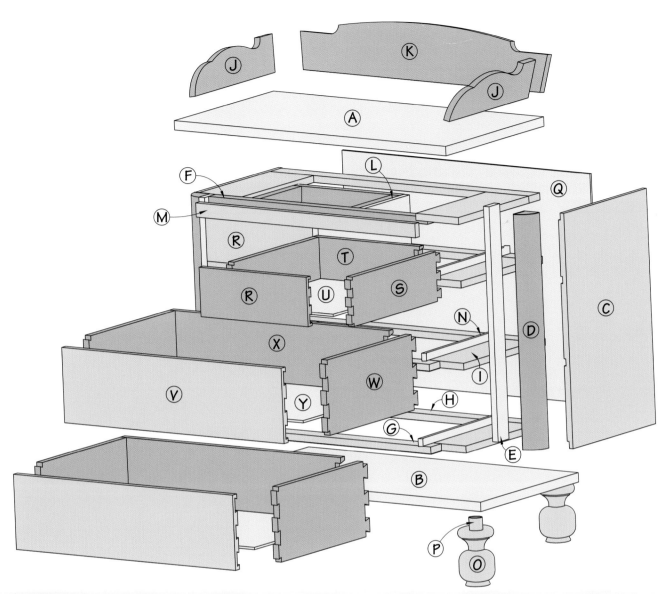

MATERIALS LIST

Colonial Washstand

No.	Letter	Item	Dimensions T W L
1	A	Top	¾″ × 18″ × 36″
1	B	Base	¾″ × 18″ × 36″
2	C	Sides	¾″ × 15¼″ × 25″
2	D	Pilasters	2″ × 2″ × 25″
2	E	Pilaster Fillers	¾″ × 2″ × 25″
1	F	Web Frames	¾″ × 1¼″ × 29″
3	G	Web Frames	¾″ × 2″ × 29″
4	H	Web Frames	¾″ × 2″ × 34½″
9	I	Web Frames	¾″ × 5¾″ × 13″
2	J	Gallery	¾″ × 5″ × 16″
1	K	Gallery	¾″ × 6″ × 33″
1	L	Drawer Partition	¾″ × 6″ × 15½″
1	M	Facing	¾″ × 1½″ × 5¼″
1	N	Trim	¾″ × 1½″ × 29″
6	O	Drawer Guides	¾″ × 1¾″ × 15″
4	P	Feet	4″ × 4″ × 6″
4	Q	Feet	¾″ × 1¼″ dowels
1	R	Back	¼″ × 24½″ × 33⅛″
2	S	Drawer Front	¾″ × 5¼″ × 14¼″
4	T	Drawer Sides	¾″ × 5¼″ × 16½″
2	U	Drawer Backs	¾″ × 4¾″ × 14¼″
2	V	Drawer Bottoms	¼″ × 16″ × 13¼″
2	W	Drawer Front	¾″ × 8″ × 29″
4	X	Drawer Sides	¾″ × 8″ × 16½″
2	Y	Drawer Backs	¾″ × 7½″ × 29″
2	Z	Drawer Bottoms	¼″ × 16″ × 27″

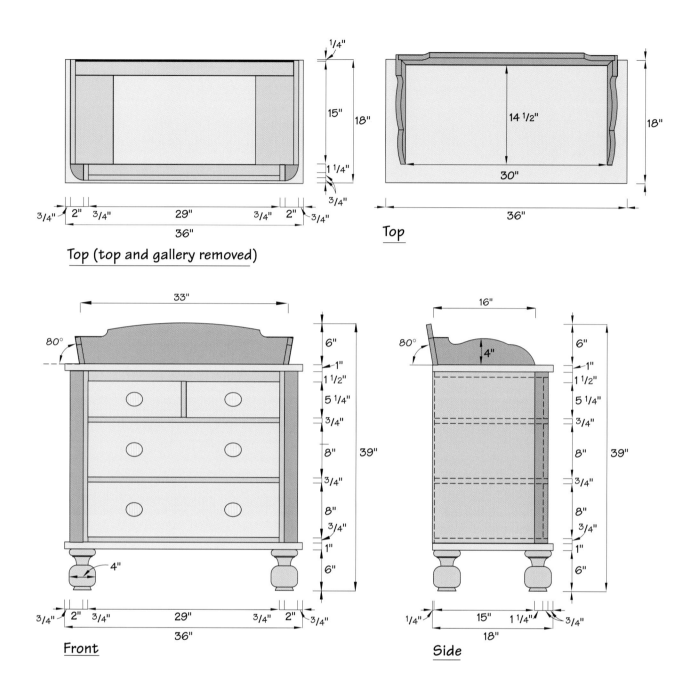

Top (top and gallery removed)

Top

Front

Side

pieces like this, however, would have been painted. I've chosen a scrubbed finish, a look I've seen often on such pieces.

Before the advent of hot and cold running water, washstands like this one would have been an essential part of most early and Victorian American bedroom suites. Towels, washcloths and other linens would have been kept in the drawers while the galleried top would have been home to a large ceramic bowl and water jug. It's a look that's often duplicated to good effect today. This washstand is a faithful copy of the one I found on Jekyll Island. I've searched the books but have not been

able to find anything quite like it. In other words, it seems to be unique.

WHAT'S IT WORTH?

For sure, an original of this period—late Colonial—if you could find one, would command a high price well into the thousands of dollars. I had no trouble selling my pine one to the trade for $450, and I received orders for several more made, not only from pine, but also from cherry and walnut. You should have no trouble selling yours privately for $600 to $800, perhaps even more.

CONSTRUCTION OUTLINE

At first glance this is a simple piece, but first glances can often be misleading. To make it you will need to use almost every tool in the shop. When it's finished it will provide you with a unique piece, as well as a real sense of achievement.

Basically, this is a small chest of drawers with turned feet, a nicely shaped gallery and rounded quarter pilasters. The web frames are offset to accommodate the pilaster and attached to the sides with glue and biscuits (dowels would work just as well). The top is made from furniture-grade pine a full 1″ thick. The kicker is also a solid piece of stock, nominally 1″ thick, upon which the carcass sits. There were no dust panels in the original. The drawers were constructed using lap joints, but, as I felt this was a quality piece, I've taken a liberty and used dovetails. The feet are glued and doweled to the kicker.

There are a couple of tricky areas: the pilasters and the construction of the carcass.

The pilasters are made from two pieces of stock, 25″ long × 2″ wide × 2″ thick. The trick here is how to achieve the quarter-round cross-section. I did it by taking pieces of stock 36½″ long × 4″ wide × 2″ thick and gluing them together—only the first six inches at either end—to make a piece 4″ × 4″. I then placed the piece in the lathe and turned off the corners to give me what was essentially an eight-sided piece—four flats and four rounded corners. At that point I removed the stock from the lathe and cut off the first six inches at either end, thus the middle section split into two halves. From there it was simply a matter of cutting one of the two halves down the middle to give me the pilasters. The two six-inch 4″ × 4″ sections? These I turned on the lathe to make two of the four required feet.

The carcass itself is fairly simple to construct; just take care that the offset web frames are accurately measured, made and dadoed into the sides. **Note:** One web frame is ¾″ narrower than the other three. Attaching the pilasters and fillers to the carcass, however, needs special attention. First you'll glue and screw the spacers, edge on, to the carcass (see top photo page 80), then glue and screw the pilasters to the spacers (see bottom photo page 80). Quite simple really.

The gallery or splash-back, as it's often called, is cut from furniture-grade pine, a full 1″ thick, and angled to slope away at 6°. The ends of the galleries are lap-jointed and secured together with glue and cut-steel masonry nails for authenticity. The hardware, which is also faith-ful to the original washstand, was bought from the Woodworker's Store.

BUILDING THE WASHSTAND

STEP 1. Cut and shape the pilasters (see Shop Tip below).

STEP 2. Cut the rest of the required pieces to size.

STEP 3. Run all the edges through the jointer.

STEP 4. Build the boards that will make the top, kicker (base) and two sides.

STEP 5. Build the four web frames as laid out in the drawing. Be careful to make one ¾″ narrower than the other three; this one will go at the top of the carcass. Also, be careful to make the offsets accurately as laid out in the drawing.

STEP 6. Take the two pieces of stock that will make the sides and cut rabbets ¾″ wide × ¼″ deep at the top and bottom edges to take the top and bottom web frames. Next, cut a rabbet down one long edge of each side ¼″ deep to receive the back—make sure you have a left and right side.

SHOP TIP
Turning Pilasters

The pilasters are an important feature of this old washstand. You might be tempted to leave them out. Don't. If you have a lathe they are quite simple and fun to make. To make your pilasters you'll need two pieces of stock 36½″ × 4″ × 2″. Apply glue to the first and last six inches of both pieces, put them together, clamp and leave overnight to cure. Find the center at each end and place the piece in the lathe. Turn the piece to round over the corners only leaving flats that measure roughly 1½″ across. While the piece is still in the lathe, sand the rounded corners smooth. Remove the piece from the lathe and cut off the first six inches at both ends; this will cause the center to fall apart into two sections, each with two ¾″ flats and a single 1½″ flat. On your table saw, split one of the pieces down the middle. This will give you two pilasters. The two 6″ sections can be turned into feet.

Glue, assemble and clamp the carcass. Note how the front center clamp is set at an angle to pull the structure square.

Glue and clamp the trim piece in place on the upper web frame, then fasten the two spacers in place on the web offsets using no. 6 screws.

STEP 7. Cut dadoes in the two side pieces as laid out in the drawing ¾″ wide × ¼″ deep to take the two center web frames.

STEP 8. Glue, assemble and clamp the four web frames to the two ends—make sure the narrower web is at the top. Square the structure, then set it aside to cure overnight.

STEP 9. Glue and screw the spacers to the webs as you see in photo above.

STEP 10. Set the pilasters in place between the spacers and the sides and mark them and the sides for biscuit slots (see photo top left page 81).

STEP 11. Cut the biscuit slots to the pilasters and side panels (see photo top right page 81).

STEP 12. Glue, biscuit and clamp the pilasters to the side panels and screw the spacers to the pilasters (see photo bottom right page 81).

STEP 13. Set the piece of stock to be used for the top trim in place against the narrower web frame and mark for biscuits.

STEP 14. Cut the biscuit slots, then glue and clamp it in place.

STEP 15. Build the drawer guide by gluing and clamping the ¾″ × ¾″ facing strip to the end grain of the piece that measures 15¾″ × 6¾″.

STEP 16. Glue and screw the drawer partition in place as laid out in the drawing and top photo page 82. You can screw downward through the upper web and upward through the one below. The partition will also double as the two center drawer guides.

STEP 17. Build the drawer guides (see Shop Tip on page 82).

STEP 18. Glue and screw the drawer guides to the carcass.

STEP 19. Turn the feet to the dimensions shown in the drawing.

STEP 20. Bore a ¾″ hole, 1″ deep, in the top center of each foot to take the dowel that will secure the foot in place on the bottom of the washstand.

STEP 21. Using a ½″ bit in your router, round over the front and side edges of the two boards that will be the top and kicker.

STEP 22. Bore four ¾″ holes at each corner of the kicker as laid out in the drawing.

STEP 23. Using one of the new polyurethane glues and four pieces of ¾″ × 1¾″ dowel, assemble the feet to the kicker (bottom photo page 82 shows all that's needed to do this). Clamp and set aside overnight to fully cure.

STEP 24. Remove the excess glue from around the feet.

STEP 25. Take the three pieces that will make the gallery and cut one end of both of the short sections and both ends of the long piece to an angle of 10° as laid out in the drawing.

Once the spacers are securely fastened to the carcass, set the pilasters in place and mark them, one side only, and the carcass for biscuit slots.

Cut the biscuit slots to the pilasters and side panels.

Take extra care to ensure the plate jointer is square to the work when milling the biscuit slots to the pilasters.

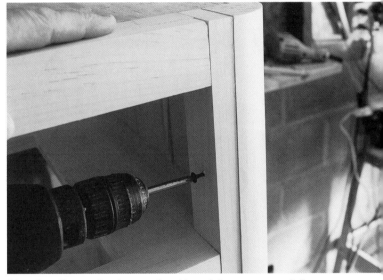

Glue the pilasters in place to the sides of the carcass and, from the inside, using glue and no. 6 screws, secure the pilasters to the spacers already screwed in place.

STEP 26. Using either your jointer or table saw, cut the bottom edges of all three pieces to 10° to give the gallery the desired tilt. Make sure you have a left and right section with the angle at the back.

STEP 27. Using the scale drawings, cut the details to the upper edges of the three gallery sections. The angle should be at the back of both end sections.

STEP 28. Cut rabbets ⅜" deep × ¾" wide to the ends of the back section of the gallery as you see in the drawing.

STEP 29. Glue, nail with cut-steel nails and clamp the side of the gallery to the back (make sure the assembly is square), and set aside overnight to fully cure.

STEP 30. From the inside, screw the kicker (base) to the lower web frame of the carcass. Elongate the holes in the carcass and use small washers under the heads of the screws to allow for movement in the kicker.

STEP 31. Set the gallery in position on the top and mark the outline lightly with a pencil.

STEP 32. Remove the gallery from the top and, using the pencil lines as a guide, bore pilot holes through the top at an angle of 10° to line up with the angle of the tilted gallery.

STEP 33. Replace the gallery and secure it in place with screws from the underside.

Using a #20 biscuit, fasten the face piece to the front edge of the drawer divider; note the offset.

Use ¾″ dowel and one of the new polyurethane glues to fasten the feet to the kicker.

STEP 34. Set the top in place on the carcass and secure with screws from the underside of the top web frame. Elongate the holes and put small washers under the heads of the screws to allow the top room to breathe.

STEP 35. Set the back in place inside the rabbets and secure in place with a few brads.

STEP 36. To build the drawers follow the procedure as laid out in the Shop Tip on page 98.

STEP 37. Go to finishing.

FINISHING

I chose a scrubbed pine look for this piece (see chapter three). First you'll need to finish sand the entire piece, then do a little light distressing and finally apply some stain. I used Minwax's Golden Pecan. It gives the pine a delicate patina that shows through the polyurethane/paint solution quite nicely for a really authentic look. When you apply the finish, simply wipe it on and then wipe it off again, leaving only the barest film of pigment over the stain.

SHOP TIP
Making Drawer Guides

I make almost all of my drawer guides by taking two pieces of stock of the appropriate length and gluing and screwing them together (see the drawing). The guide piece should be made from a stock ¾″ × 1″ and the support from a section ¾″ × 2″— sometimes it will need to be wider. Glue the edge of the guide section, assemble it to the support section and secure the resulting assembly with a couple of screws.

Chapter 13

Plantation Desk

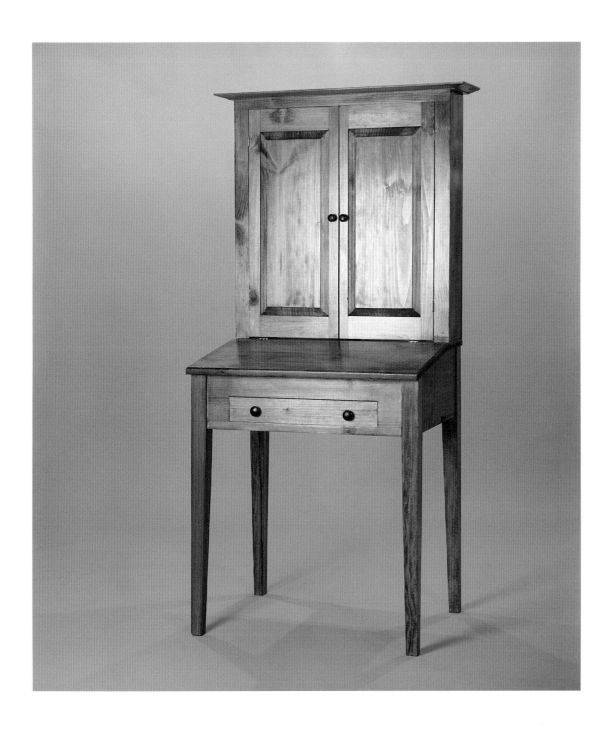

This type of desk first appeared around the turn of the nineteenth century. While the masters were turning out elaborate drop or fall-front secretaries, country furniture builders developed this much simpler style called a plantation or cupboard desk. Some were more elaborate than others. Some Shaker versions had fall-fronts that revealed several small drawers and a couple of pigeon holes: it was

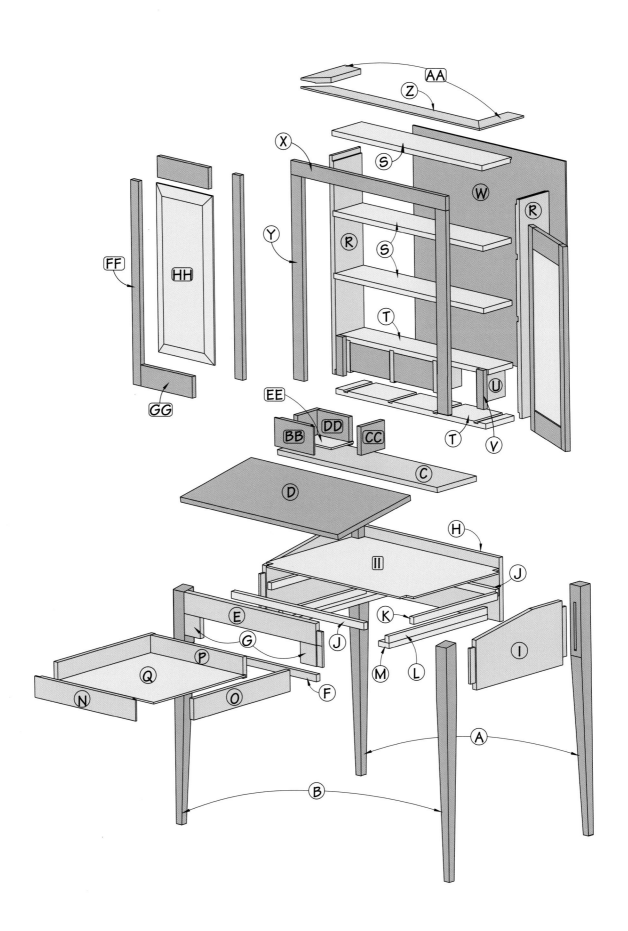

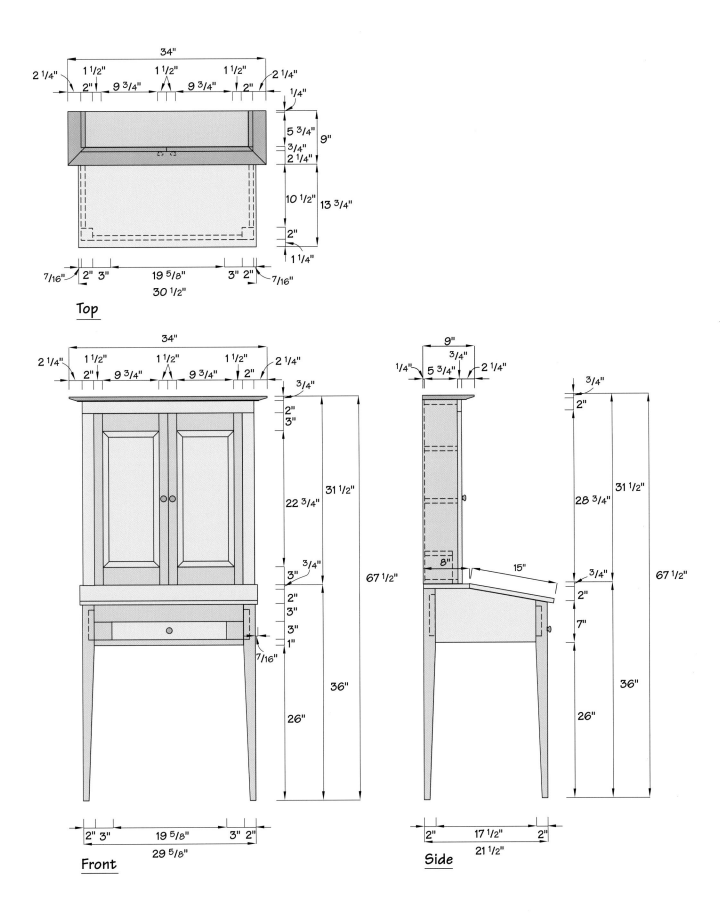

Top

Front

Side

Plantation Desk

No.	Letter	Item	Dimensions T W L
2	A	Legs	2½″ × 2½″ × 35¼″
2	B	Legs	2½″ × 2½″ × 33″
1	C	Lid	1″ × 8″ × 30½″
1	D	Lid	1″ × 15″ × 30½″
1	E	*Front	¾″ × 3″ × 27⅝″
1	F	*Front	¾″ × 1″ × 27⅝″
2	G	*Front	¾″ × 3″ × 4″
1	H	Back	¼″ × 9″ × 27⅝″
2	I	Sides	¾″ × 9″ × 19½″
2	J	Cleats	¾″ × 1″ × 25½″
2	K	Cleats	¾″ × 1″ × 17″
2	L	Cleats	¾″ × ¾″ × 17½″
2	M	Cleats	¾″ × 2″ × 17½″
1	N	Drawer Front	¾″ × 3″ × 19⅝″
2	O	Drawer Sides	¾″ × 3″ × 19″
1	P	Drawer Back	¾″ × 2½″ × 18⅝″
1	Q	Drawer Bottom	¼″ × 18½″ × 18⅝″
2	R	Upper Sides	¾″ × 6″ × 30¾″
3	S	Shelves	¾″ × 6″ × 28½″
2	T	Drawer Section	¾″ × 5″ × 28½″
2	U	Dividers	½″ × 5″ × 4½″
2	V	Spacers	¾″ × 1″ × 5½″
2	W	Back	¼″ × 31″ × 30″
1	X	Trim	¾″ × 2″ × 29½″
2	Y	Trim	¾″ × 2″ × 28¾″
1	Z	Crown	¾″ × 3″ × 34″
2	AA	Crown	¾″ × 3″ × 9″

Upper Drawers

No.	Letter	Item	Dimensions T W L
3	BB	Drawer Fronts	¾″ × 4″ × 7½″
6	CC	Drawer Sides	¾″ × 4″ × 4¾″
2	DD	Drawer Backs	¾″ × 4½″ × 6½″
2	EE	Drawer Bottoms	¼″ × 4″ × 6½″
2	FF	Door Stiles	¾″ × 1½″ × 28¾″
2	GG	Door Rails	¾″ × 3″ × 9¾″
2	HH	Door Panels	¾″ × 10¾″ × 24½″
2	II	Recessed Bottom	⅜″ × 17½″ × 26⅝″

*Includes for tenon

essentially a simple form of the more traditional secretary. The plantation or cupboard desk had a lift-top and was basically a cupboard on a frame. I have opted for this 1810 version: the plantation desk.

Some of these desks were made from hardwood—cherry, maple or walnut—but most were made from pine. Some had glass doors, some panel doors and some no doors at all. A few had a drawer below the writing section, as does ours.

WHAT'S IT WORTH?

An original, if you could find one, might sell for as much as $4,000, and I've seen reproductions sell for $1,500 and up. The cost in materials is about $70, including hardware. It takes about twenty hours, on and off, for me to make one of these desks. That's because I've made a number of them. You can expect to spend at least thirty hours, perhaps more, and to sell it to the trade for between $500 and $600. You could get much more if you sell it privately. They, in turn, will retail it anywhere from $950 to $1,250. I've seen much simpler versions retailing for just as much.

CONSTRUCTION OUTLINE

As simple as most of these desks were, the somewhat challenging construction should be well within the capabilities of most moderately experienced hobbyists. There are one or two tricky areas you should be aware of. The top section has three small drawers set back from the shelves to allow room for the small pulls when the doors are closed. The dividers are made from 1/2 stock, which means you'll need to do either some planing or resawing.

The lift-top of the lower section slants forward at an angle of 10°. This means there are lots of angles to cut, the front legs are shorter than those at the rear and the tops are cut at an angle of 10°, the sides are also angled at 10°, so is the top edge of the front and the rear edge of the lift-top.

The bottom of the desk compartment is made from ⅜″ plywood secured to four cleats, and the drawer runners and guides are secured to two more cleats. These are all fairly simple to install and should be no cause for concern. As the plantation desk was basically a simple, homemade piece, the drawers are constructed using rabbets, glue and cut nails. The 1½″ cut-steel masonry nails you can buy at most hardware stores fill this task nicely and look quite authentic. You could, of course, use blind dovetail construction, but the finished product, while looking much nicer, would not be authentic.

The legs are cut from 8/4 stock and tapered on two adjacent sides to 2°; be sure you make two left and two right, the tapers all facing inward and each other. The sides, front and back are secured to the legs using mortise-and-tenon joints. I used one of the new polyurethane glues to achieve this. I like the way the glue expands to fill the joint.

The top and lid of the lower section (two pieces—lift section and fixed) is made from 1″ furniture-grade pine. You could, of course, use the same good old shelving board from which the rest of the piece is made. The front of the lower section is made from four pieces of stock. The crown is simply made from nominal 1″ stock, laid flat and cut just like a raised panel.

BUILDING THE DESK

STEP 1. Cut all the pieces to size, and cut the ⅜″-thick plywood bottom roughly to shape; you can make final adjustments later.

STEP 2. Build the board for the lid.

STEP 3. Using four pieces of stock, build the front of the lower section as laid out in the drawing.

STEP 4. Mill the dadoes in both sides of the top section as laid out in the drawing.

STEP 5. Glue, assemble and toenail the shelves to the sides of the upper section. Clamp, make sure the structure is completely square, then set it aside to fully cure.

STEP 6. Mill the tops of the two front legs—the two short ones—to an angle of 10°.

STEP 7. Cut the two sides of the lower section to shape as laid out in the drawing; the slope is 10°.

STEP 8. Starting 10″ from the top of the two rear legs, and 8″ from the top of the two front legs, using either your table saw or jointer, taper two adjacent sides of all four legs, making sure you have two left and two right.

STEP 9. Cut the mortises to the tapered sides of all four legs as laid out in the drawing. **Note:** The mortises that will take the tenons of the front section are different from those that will take the sides and back. Also the 10° slope to the top of the front legs should slant forward—toward you.

STEP 10. Mill the tenons to the front, sides and back of the lower section as laid out in the drawing.

STEP 11. Dry assemble the lower section to ensure you have a good fit. If all is well, disassemble the piece, then glue, reassemble, clamp, ensure the structure is square, then set it aside until the glue is fully cured.

STEP 12. Glue and screw the two guide supports to the back and front of the inside of the lower section as laid out in the drawing.

STEP 13. Glue and screw the four cleats that will support the bottom of the desk cavity to the inside of the lower section as laid out in the drawing.

Use a movable square to set the angle to the back fence of your jointer.

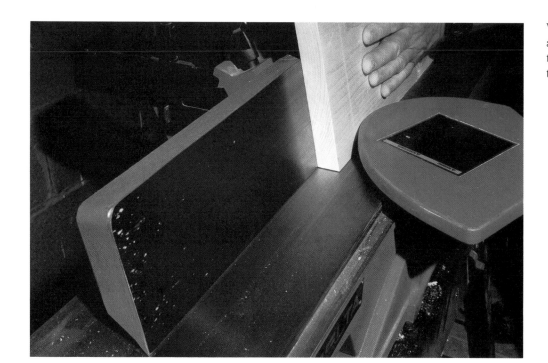

When you've set the correct angle, use your jointer to mill the angle to the back edge of the desk lid.

You'll need to build a simple jig to cut the angle to the top of the two front legs.

STEP 14. Build the drawer guides and fit them to the two supports.

STEP 15. Make any final adjustments to the ⅜″ plywood cavity bottom, then using small brass screws, fasten it in place on the four cleats above the drawer cavity.

STEP 16. Take both sections of the lid to the router and round over the two ends of the rear section and both ends and front of the lift section.

STEP 17. Take the lid to the jointer or table saw and mill the back edge to an angle of 10° so that it will fit

nicely against the rear section.

STEP 18. Mark out and cut mortises for 1¼″ brass butt hinges to both sections as laid out in the drawing.

STEP 19. Using two 1¼″ brass butt hinges, assemble the two sections of the lid together.

STEP 20. Carefully set the assembled lid section in place on top of the desk, then glue and screw the rear section of the lid in place on the flat area at the rear.

STEP 21. Returning to the upper section, lay it flat on the

To work your door panels, set the table saw blade to cut at an angle between 15° and 17°. The blade should just break through the surface, leaving a nice, clean step that will define the panel.

Attach the trim to the upper section with biscuits. Mark the side of the cupboard section and the edge of the trim, and then carefully mill the slots.

bench, put the trim in place and mark for biscuit slots. If you don't use biscuits you can glue, clamp and nail the pieces in place.

STEP 22. Remove the trim and mill the biscuit slots.

STEP 23. Glue and clamp the trim in place. If you've used nails, now's the time to set the heads and fill the holes.

STEP 24. Glue and clamp the two small fillers in place between the trim and drawer section as you see in the drawing and photo above (bottom).

STEP 25. Take the three pieces that will make up the crown to the table saw, which should be set to cut at an angle of 17°. Place the stock on edge and mill the crown just as you would if you were making a raised-panel door (see top photo above).

STEP 26. Cut the three sections of the crown to their final dimensions, then miter the ends to 45°.

STEP 27. Glue and screw the crown in place to the top of the cupboard section. Glue the miters together.

Try this setup to make milling the mortises for the hinges easier. The extra support provided by the top board will enable you to mill an accurate mortise.

STEP 28. Build the two doors as laid out in the drawing and the Shop Tip on page 91.

STEP 29. Mark the doors and opening for 1¼″ brass butt hinges as laid out in the drawing, but do not fit them yet.

STEP 30. Set the cupboard section carefully in place on the rear flat section of the desk and carefully secure them together using no. 8 × 1¾″ screws. If you've used ¾″ stock for the lid you need to use 1½″ screws.

STEP 31. Build the three small drawers for the cupboard section as laid out in the drawing.

STEP 32. Build the drawer for the desk section as laid out in the drawing.

STEP 33. Finish sand all the completed sections and drawers.

STEP 34. Apply a coat of stain to all sections of the desk and drawers.

STEP 35. After finishing is complete you can attach the knobs to the doors and drawers and fit the doors to the cupboard section.

FINISHING

I kept things very simple for this piece. After doing a little light distressing and applying a medium stain, I applied eight coats of seedlac mixed to a three-pound cut. This gave the piece a deep, almost dark golden shine. The final step was to apply a couple of coats of beeswax—ummmm, nice.

SHOP TIP
Building a Raised Panel Door

Today, most people use a router table and an expensive set of bits to mill the pieces for a raised panel door. True, you can mill some pretty edges, as well as curved tops and the like, but to me, the expense is not worth the result. The heavy bits require a three-horse router or a shaper, the bits cost a fortune and the method requires more time than I have available. I prefer, instead, the old-fashioned look: square door frames and flat, beveled panels. They are quick and simple to make, especially with a little practice. I can make a set of four doors, complete, in a only a couple of hours. The way I do it is somewhat controversial, but it works for me. The method is as follows:

1. Begin by cutting your rails and stiles exactly to length.

2. Use either your router with a $^5/_{16}$" straight-cutting bit or your table saw to mill $^3/_8$"-deep grooves to the inner edges of the rails. The cut runs the entire length of the rails, and stops $2^3/_4$" short from both ends of the stiles. I use my router table with the stops marked on a piece of masking tape that shows just above the stock.

3. Once you've cut the slots, lay out the rails and stiles and mark for biscuit slots. You can use lap joints if you like, but you'll need to adjust the length of the rails to maintain the outer dimensions of the doors.

4. Mill the biscuit slots.

5. Dry fit the rails and stiles and measure the width and height between the grooves to get the true size of the panels.

6. Sand the rails and stiles smooth and stain the inner edges. It's much easier to stain them before than after assembly.

7. Glue and clamp the rails and stiles, *one side only*, dry fit the other, ensure all is square, then set them aside until the glue is fully cured.

8. If necessary, build the boards that will make the panels and trim them to size.

9. Set your table saw to cut at an angle of 17°, and the rip fence at $^1/_4$" and mill the bevels to the edges of the panels. The tip of the blade should just break through the surface of the stock, leaving a small step and nice clean lines.

10. Sand the panels smooth, paying close attention to the bevels, and then apply the stain.

11. When the glue is fully cured, remove the clamps from the frames, and remove the dry-fitted stiles.

12. Slide the panels into place in the now open frames, glue and clamp the remaining stiles in place, and set the completed doors aside to allow the glue to fully cure.

13. Either round-over or break the outer edges.

14. Do any necessary sanding to the joints, then the finish sanding and, finally, complete the staining.

Chapter 14

New England Pantry

T o think of a pantry is to think of a small, cold room beyond the kitchen where food, ingredients, utensils and other such culinary items are kept. Usually they're associated with large houses and butlers, but that's something of a misconception brought about by fiction writers such as Agatha Christie. I grew up in a house with a pantry. I remember it as a narrow, cold, dark place, lined with shelves and

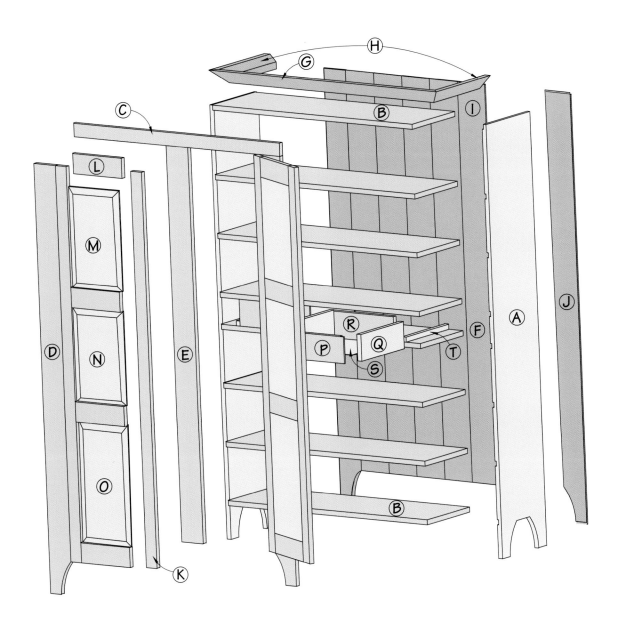

with a fine screen covering the tiny window. Here in America, in Colonial times, few settlers could afford homes with room enough for a pantry, so the pantry cupboard evolved. Always kept in the kitchen, it was a simple affair with two doors the full height of the piece, small legs to keep the food off the floor, shelves and perhaps a couple of drawers inside. They were almost always painted, often in bright colors, even white, and ours, a copy of one made in Pennsylvania around 1800, is no exception.

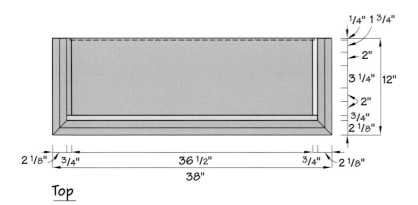

Top

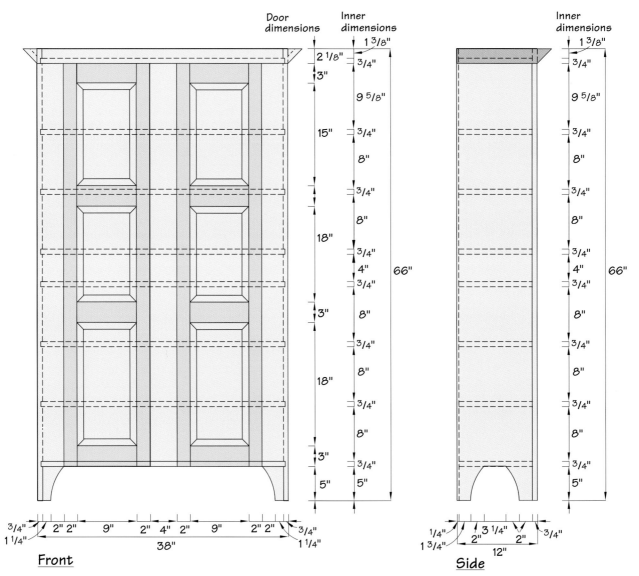

Front

Side

Door dimensions

Inner dimensions

Inner dimensions

New England Pantry

No.	Letter	Item	Dimensions T W L
2	A	Sides	¾″ × 11¼″ × 66″
8	B	Shelves, Drawer Support, Bottom and Top	¾″ × 11¼″ × 26″
1	C	Trim	¾″ × 2″ × 38″
2	D	Trim	¾″ × 4″ × 64″
1	E	Trim	¾″ × 4″ × 59″
6	F	Shelf Cleats	¾″ × ¾″ × 3″
1	G	Crown	¾″ × 2″ × 3″
2	H	Crown	¾″ × 3″ × 13″
2	I	Back	¾″ × 5½″ × 66″
5	J	Back	¾″ × 5½″ × 61″
4	K	Door Stiles	¾″ × 2″ × 59″
4	L	Door Rails	¾″ × 3″ × 9″
4	M	Door Upper Panels	¾″ × 1½″ × 9½″
4	N	Door Center Panels	¾″ × 14½″ × 9½″
4	O	Door Lower Panels	¾″ × 18½″ × 9½″
4	P	Drawer Fronts	¾″ × 4″ × 13″
4	Q	Drawer Sides	¾″ × 4″ × 10″
4	R	Drawer Backs	¾″ × 3½″ × 11½″
4	S	Drawer Bottoms	¾″ × 12″ × 10½″
4	T	Drawer Guides	¾″ × 1″ × 11″

WHAT'S IT WORTH?

A piece like this should easily sell for around $350 or more, depending upon the area and outlet.

CONSTRUCTION OUTLINE

This is another fairly simple project. With the exception of the raised-panel doors, construction is quite straightforward.

The sides are made from single pieces of stock, dadoed to take the shelves, of which there are eight including the top, bottom and drawer support. The trim is fastened to the carcass with glue and nails as was done on the original, but you can use biscuits and glue if you like. If you do decide to use biscuits, you'll also need to use cleats and screws on the inside to hold the center trim to the shelves (these are allowed for in the materials list). The crown is constructed from three pieces of stock, mitered, glued and screwed to the top. The back is made from seven pieces of ¾″ pine stock butted together, similar to what you would find on an original piece, but you could use a single piece of lauan plywood. The drawers are set back just enough to allow room for the doors to close over the pulls and are made using simple lap joints, glue and cut-steel nails. The two doors are of raised-panel construction—the panels are irregular and sized to meet the demands of good design—and secured to the carcass with reproduction "H" hinges, stripped of paint and aged for authenticity. For the finish I chose first to stain the piece, then apply a couple of coats of dark green paint. You can expect to spend several weekends on this project.

BUILDING THE PANTRY

STEP 1. Cut all the pieces to size.

STEP 2. Mill the dadoes to the two sides as laid out in the drawing, then mark and cut out the details for the feet. (It's best to use your jigsaw for this operation.)

STEP 3. Sand both faces of the sides smooth and apply your chosen stain.

STEP 4. Sand both surfaces of all of the shelves, drawer support, bottom and top, then apply your stain.

STEP 5. Using glue, clamps and toenails, assemble the carcass. Check the diagonals to make sure the structure is square, then set it aside overnight or until the glue is fully cured.

STEP 6. Sand all four pieces of trim smooth and apply stain.

STEP 7. There are a couple of ways to attach the trim to the carcass. You can glue, nail and clamp as I did, and as was done on the original, or you can biscuit them on. If you decide to use nails, skip the next four steps. Just set the nail heads and use a dark filler to cover the holes. They'll still show, but that's good; country carpenters 200 hundred years ago were not so particular as we are today. If you decide to use biscuits, remove the clamps from the carcass, lay it on its back, set the trim in place and mark for the slots. It's best if you allow 8″ or 9″ between biscuits.

STEP 8. Mill the biscuit slots.

STEP 9. Glue and clamp the trim in place and set the structure aside until the glue is fully cured.

You'll need to reinforce the butt joints between the two pieces of stock that make up the sides with biscuits or dowels. Ideally, these should be placed 8″ to 10″ apart.

For accuracy, when milling the dadoes, you can clamp two sides together and do both at once. You'll need to make sure your T square is exactly 90° to the sides, of course. You can make sure by measuring the setting at both ends of the square in relation to the top or bottom. Whichever you use, top or bottom, use the same reference point for each dado you mill.

STEP 10. Using no. 6 × 1⅝″ screws, glue and screw the small cleats to the front underside of the six shelves, including the drawer support, the top and the upper front of the bottom.

STEP 11. Using no. 6 × 1⅝″ screws, from the inside, glue and screw the center trim to the carcass. You'll need to drill pilot holes first. Make sure it is square to the outer trim and the openings match exactly.

STEP 12. Use either your router with a 5⁄16″ straight-

cutting bit or your table saw to mill 5⁄16″-deep grooves to the inner edges of the rails and stiles that will make up the two doors.

STEP 13. Lay out the rails and stiles and mark for biscuit slots. You can use lap joints if you like, but you'll need to adjust the length of the rails to maintain the outer dimensions of the doors.

STEP 14. Mill the biscuit slots.

STEP 15. Dry fit the rails and stiles and measure the width and height between the grooves to ensure the panels will fit properly.

STEP 16. If necessary, trim the panels to size.

STEP 17. Sand the rails and stiles smooth and apply your stain.

STEP 18. Glue and clamp the rails and stiles, *one side only*, dry fit the other, ensure all is square, then set them aside until the glue is fully cured.

STEP 19. Set your table saw to cut at an angle of 17° and the rip fence at ¼″, and mill the bevels to the edges of the panels. The tip of the blade should just break through the surface of the stock, leaving a small step and nice clean lines.

STEP 20. Sand the panels smooth, paying close attention to the bevels, then apply the stain.

STEP 21. When the glue is fully cured, remove the clamps from the frames, and remove the dry-fitted stiles.

Use a compass and pencil to mark the detail for the feet. You'll find your jigsaw the best tool for removing the waste.

For strength, glue and then toenail screw the shelves into the dadoes. When you've squared the carcass, and the glue has fully cured, you'll have a structure that's rock solid.

When you're putting the drawers together, drill pilot holes to ease the passage of the rather bulky cut-steel nails.

SHOP TIP
Fitting a Door

Fitting a door, or pair of doors, can often be something of a trial, especially if the frame or, in the case of a raised panel assembly, the door, is slightly out of square. Yep, it happens even to the best. This is the easy way to do it.

First, I always make my doors just a little larger than the opening, say ¼". The purists may say I'm cheating. Not so, just practical. You can always take a little off; you can't add a little on if you make a mistake. I don't have time and money enough to remake a raised panel door, or even a solid one for that matter.

Next I set the door in the opening and determine how to remove so it will fit closely.

Now, I remove excess material from the length of the door on the table saw. To remove it from the width I use the jointer.

If the door or opening is out of square, I cut the door to the correct length. Then, using the tapering technique described on page 87, I take the door to the jointer, set the machine to cut at a depth of ⅟₃₂", and make as many passes as necessary to remove enough material for the door to fit the opening. Usually two passes are quite enough.

STEP 22. Slide the panels into place in the now open frames, glue and clamp the remaining stiles in place and set the completed doors aside to allow the glue to fully cure.

STEP 23. Glue and screw the four drawer guides in place, making sure they are square to the front openings.

STEP 24. Build the drawers as laid out in the drawing and Shop Tip at right.

STEP 25. Go to the finishing process below.

STEP 26. Attach the doors to the carcass.

STEP 27. Attach the hardware to the doors and drawers.

STEP 28. Set the swivel catches in place and fasten with no. $6 \times 1\frac{5}{8}''$ screws.

FINISHING

Your staining is all done, so all that's left is to do the appropriate distressing, painting and aging. First, do some light distressing around the trim, the corners and the edges of the doors, a little heavier around the feet, and then some final sanding with a fine-grit paper. Next, apply a couple of coats of polyurethane, then a couple of coats of a dark green paint of your choice. Allow the paint to dry completely, at least forty-eight hours, then go to the rubbing-down stage. You'll want the stain to show through in the areas that would be subject to heavy wear—around door edges, doorknobs, swivel catches, corners, outer edges of the carcass and around the feet. Next you'll need to complete the illusion by applying an antiquing glaze. I used pigmented paint thinner, but pigmented, diluted, water-based polyurethane would do the job just as well. Finally, you'll need to apply a coat of clear polyurethane for protection.

SHOP TIP
Simple Drawers

Most of the drawers you'll find in this book are made using very simple construction methods: lap joints, glue and cut-steel nails. This was the method most often used by the colonial craftsmen when working with pine. Pine tends to breathe, expand, shrink and swell, more so than the hardwoods, therefore lap joints were preferred to dovetails. I use cut-steel nails simply because they look more authentic than finishing nails. The method is as follows:

1. Cut all the pieces to size. The back of the drawer will be $\frac{1}{2}''$ narrower than the sides and front.

2. Rabbet the inside edges of the drawer fronts, $\frac{3}{4}''$ wide and $\frac{1}{2}''$ deep, leaving $\frac{1}{4}''$ of material on the outer face. I use my Delta tenoning jig to cut the cheeks, and my table saw to cut shoulders.

3. Rabbet the drawer sides on one end only, $\frac{3}{4}''$ wide and $\frac{1}{2}''$ deep, leaving $\frac{1}{4}''$ of material on the outer face.

4. Using one of the drawer backs as a template, set the table saw rip fence and blade to cut at a depth of $\frac{1}{4}''$. Cut slots in both sides and the front to accept the $\frac{1}{4}''$ plywood bottom. Cut once, then move the rip fence out $\frac{1}{8}''$ and cut again. Be sure you make two left- and two right-hand sides.

5. Assemble the drawer's using glue and cut steel nails, check the diagonals to ensure they are square, then clamp and set them aside until the glue is fully cured.

6. Fit the drawers bottom and secure it in place with a couple of brads to the back edge.

7. Attach the hardware.

8. Do any necessary finish sanding, break all the sharp edges and you're done.

C h a p t e r 1 5

Eighteenth-Century Huntboard

The huntboard has its origins in Europe, England in particular. It was a functional piece of furniture, never the fine piece it's turned out to be today. Found mostly in the kitchens of the great houses, both in the American South and in England, it was used to serve buffet-style refreshments to the men returning from the fox hunt, covered in mud and dirt; they are still used in England for that purpose today. I remember

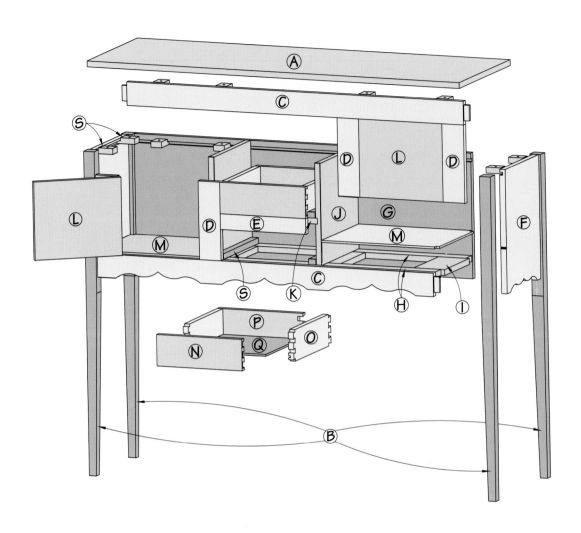

MATERIALS LIST

Huntboard

No.	Letter	Item	Dimensions T W L
4	A	Top	¾″ × 17″ × 52″
4	B	Legs	1 ½″ × 1½″ × 41¼″
2	C	Frame Parts	¾″ × 3″ × 48½″
4	D	Frame Parts	¾″ × 3″ × 10″
1	E	Frame Parts	¾″ × 2″ × 12″
2	F	Sides	¾″ × 11¼″ × 16″
1	G	*Back	¾″ × 16″ × 48½″
2	H	Frame Parts	¾″ × 2″ × 47″
4	I	Frame Parts	¾″ × 4″ × 11¼″
2	J	drw. section	¾″ × 12½″ × 13″

No.	Letter	Item	Dimensions T W L
1	K	drw. section	¾″ × 12⅛″ × 14⅝″
2	L	Cupboard Doors	¾″ × 10″ × 11¾″
2	M	Cupboard Bottoms	¼″ × 12″ × 16″
2	N	Fronts	¾″ × 4″ × 12″
4	O	Sides	¾″ × 4″ × 12½″
2	P	Backs	¾″ × 3½″ × 10½″
2	Q	Bottoms	¼″ × 12⅜″ × 10½″
4	R	Drawer Guides	¾″ × 1″ × 12″

*Includes Tenons

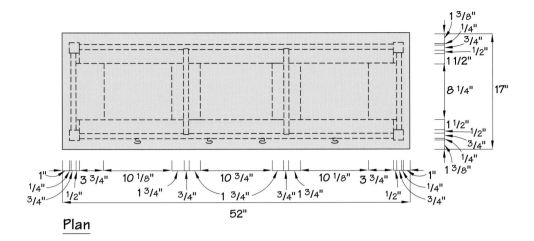

Plan

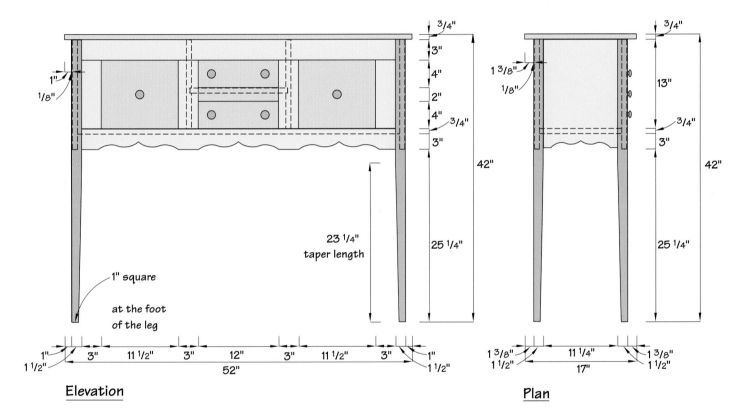

Elevation

Plan

many times back in the late seventies when I was a member of the North Cotswold Hunt, eating grand goodies—cold cuts, roast pheasant, jugged hare and the like—from a very large huntboard in the great kitchen of an old stone manor house just west of Stratford-upon-Avon. The kitchen had a huge, wood-fired (now oil-fired) range and a massive farmhouse table big enough to seat at least a dozen with long benches instead of chairs. It was quite an experience to see the men in black or red coats (called pinks), the ladies in long, black, sidesaddle habits and top hats, the great room misty with cigar smoke and filled with the noise of a dozen or so people reliving the events of the day; grand

times, for sure. Anyway, back to the huntboard.

The typical southern huntboard, found from Virginia south and as far west as Kentucky, is 4′ × 6′ with a flat top, square corners and plain or beaded edges. The front of the case is straight and contains either a central cupboard flanked by two deep drawers, two central shallow drawers flanked by cupboards or two deep half-width drawers. The drawer fronts are usually plain and fitted with round brass or wooden knobs. The doors are usually plain and flat—they might also have sunken panels—fitted with brass pendant ring handles or turned wooden knobs. The case is supported by four or six long, tapered square legs—a la Hepplewhite—or ring-and-baluster turned. The height varies from 42″ to 52″. Almost all were simple, plantation-made pieces of southern hard pine, circa 1785 to 1830, but a few were made of walnut during the same period. Ours is a copy of one illustrated in Hepplewhite's 1788 *Cabinet-Maker and Upholster's Guide*. It has the classic Hepplewhite legs and two central drawers flanked by square cupboards.

WHAT'S IT WORTH?

An original would fetch several thousands of dollars at auction. Yours should easily sell for between $400 and $600. Having said that, it's a historic piece, one you won't often see outside of a museum, a conversation starter, and it might be worth hanging on to.

CONSTRUCTION OUTLINE

With the exception of a few tricky areas the construction of our huntboard is fairly straightforward. The dimensions are 52″ long × 17″ deep × 42″ high. The front and back are mortised and tenoned to the legs. The front is basically a frame constructed using seven pieces of stock; the sides are solid and made from two pieces of stock jointed together and biscuited to the legs. The back is also solid and built from two pieces of stock. The bottoms of the cupboards are made from ¼″ lauan plywood over a lower frame joined to the carcass with biscuits. The doors are set with mortised brass butt hinges. The drawers are constructed using dovetail and butt joints. The legs are made from blanks cut from a 2″ × 12″ pine floor joist and tapered down from 1¾″ nominal to 1″ square at the tips, then mortised to take the front and back tenons; biscuit slots are cut in the other quadrant to receive the sides.

The tricky areas? First, remember accurate measuring and cutting are essential. Follow the instructions for the parts that are offset to accommodate the legs and the drawer assembly. The biscuit slots that join the lower frame to the front and back take a little thought, some accurate marking and using the machine in an unusual position. The internal drawer assembly itself must be accurately made, and the final assembly of all the parts is something of a puzzle, so you should follow exactly the order in which they are put together as laid out in the step-by-step instruction.

BUILDING THE HUNTBOARD

STEP 1. Cut and shape the legs. You can do the tapering either on your jointer, as I did, or on your table saw. Start the taper 18″ from the top of the leg. Make sure you have two left and two right legs.

STEP 2. Cut the rest of the parts as laid out in the materials list.

STEP 3. Build the boards needed for the top, sides and back.

STEP 4. Take the seven parts needed to construct the front and set the rest aside.

STEP 5. Using your jointer, clean up all the edges.

STEP 6. Cut the cyma curves to the lower edge of the bottom rail.

STEP 7. Lay out and mark the front for biscuits—be sure to number each joint—and cut the slots; you can use dowels if you like.

STEP 8. Cut tenons (2″ long × ⅜″ wide × ¾″ deep) on the two long rails.

STEP 9. Mark the two front legs for matching mortises—the edge of the mortise should be ⁷⁄₁₆″ from the front edge for a ¼″ reveal between leg and frame—and cut.

STEP 10. Dry fit the frame and legs.

STEP 11. Disassemble, then glue and clamp the frame, making sure the assembly is square. Do not attach the legs yet.

STEP 12. Cut tenons (2″ long × ⅜″ wide × ¾″ deep) on the ends of the back as shown in the drawing; mark and cut matching mortises to the two back legs, ⁷⁄₁₆″ from the outer edges.

STEP 13. Dry fit the back to the legs; do not glue yet.

STEP 14. Lay out the sides and legs and mark both for biscuits. You'll need to prop the pieces (see top right photo page 103). Be sure to number each joint. You can use dowels if you like.

STEP 15. If it's not already set, set your plate jointer to cut slots in the center (⅜″) of long edges of the sides, and cut the slots.

STEP 16. Reset your plate jointer to cut slots ⅝″ from the outside edge of the legs. This will give you a ¼″ reveal between legs and board and will match the front and rear.

STEP 17. Reset your plate joiner to its original position.

STEP 18. Dry fit the sides to the legs, but do not fix permanently yet.

STEP 19. Cut the slots to the front frame, back and sides to receive buttons for attaching the top to the carcass.

STEP 20. Mark and cut stopped dadoes on the inside of the front and back as laid out in the drawing. These should be ³/₁₆″ deep and a little more than 13″ long.

STEP 21. Take the three pieces that make up the inner drawer assembly, mark the sides for dadoes as laid out in the drawing and cut the dadoes. These should be ³/₁₆″ deep. Do not glue up yet.

STEP 22. Lay out the six pieces that make up the lower internal frame. Be sure to offset the two end pieces, as laid out in the drawing, to accommodate the legs. Mark for biscuits numbering each joint, and cut the slots.

STEP 23. Glue, assemble and clamp the lower internal frame, making sure the assembly is square.

STEP 24. Mark the inside of the front and back to receive the lower frame. Use a pencil and draw a line the entire length of the back 13″ from the top. The line you'll mark on the inside of the front should run flush with the upper edge of the lower rail.

Cut the cyma curves on your band saw in two sections.

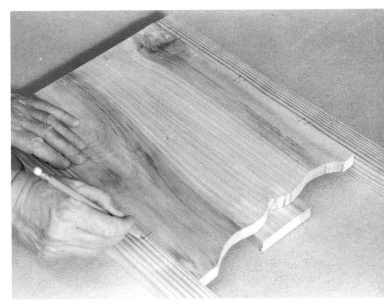

Prop the side into the correct position in relation to the legs before marking for the biscuit slots.

Use your router and a ¾″ mortise bit to cut the stopped dadoes to the inside of the front frame and the back; note the finished dado to the right.

Offset the shelf of the drawer assembly by ³/₁₆″.

STEP 25. Mark the front, back and lower frame for biscuits.

STEP 26. Cut the biscuit slots.

STEP 27. Sand all of the pieces smooth, ready for final assembly.

STEP 28. Glue, assemble and clamp the carcass together in the following order. It's essential you follow the schedule as laid out below. If not, you'll get into a mess.

28A. Glue and clamp the front frame to the left and right front legs. Leave overnight to cure.

28B. Glue and clamp the back to the left and right back legs. Leave overnight to cure.

28C. Lay the front section flat with inside up, then glue and fit the lower frame to the front.

28D. Glue and fit the sides to the front legs.

28E. Glue and fit the back and rear legs section to the sides and lower frame, then clamp, making sure the entire assembly is square, and leave overnight to cure.

28F. Glue and assemble the three pieces that make up the drawer section, making sure to offset the shelf by ³⁄₁₆″ at both front and back (see drawing and bottom right photo page 81); do not clamp.

28G. While the glue is still wet, slide the drawer assembly into the stopped dadoes on the inside of the front and back of the carcass all the way down until it touches the lower frame; there's no need to glue the drawer assembly in place.

28H. Cut and fit the plywood cupboard bottoms.

STEP 29. Cut and fit the drawer guides to the drawer assembly and the lower frame.

STEP 30. Using your router and a ½″ roundover bit, cut beads to the upper edges of the front and sides of the top, sand it smooth and set it aside for finishing.

STEP 31. By hand, lightly sand the entire piece ready for finishing.

STEP 32. Using blind dovetails at the front and butt joints at the rear, assemble the drawers—use ¼″ lauan plywood for the bottoms—and attach the knobs.

STEP 33. Cut mortises in the outer edges of the two cupboard doors, dry fit the doors to the frame, attach the knobs and set them aside for finishing.

STEP 34. Sand the doors and drawers smooth, ready for finishing.

FINISHING

I have taken liberties with the finish. Rather than the naturally aged and distressed look with a low-luster sheen you would expect to see on a piece like this, I have grain-painted mine. However, if you would like a look more in keeping with place and use, you can do some light distressing, stain the piece—it should be quite dark—then finish it off with a couple of coats of seedlac and two more of Minwax Antique Oil buffed to nice luster.

To grain paint the piece, first do a little light distressing, then follow the basic instructions in chapter three.

Choose a nice, light-colored paint for the base coat and a much darker brown color for the glaze—I used salmon pink for the base coat and burnt sienna for the glaze. To make the pattern, I used a small potato with an interesting shape and cut it in half. I simply pressed the flat section of half of the potato into the glaze, then lifted it off, repeating the process over and over to make the pattern. To finish, I applied a couple of coats of semigloss polyurethane.

Finally, attach the top to the carcass using eight buttons (you can use screws and pocket holes if you like), one to each side and three each along the front and back, and attach the cupboard doors.

Chapter 16

Early Nineteenth-Century Pie Safe

T he pie safe was a simple utility piece kept in the kitchen of most early American homes from the mid-1700s on. It was where the cook or farmer's wife stored her baked goods. Most had three shelves and either one or two drawers placed above the doors, although some had the drawers below the doors instead. The doors themselves had either wire screens or, after 1800, pierced tin panels to allow heat from freshly

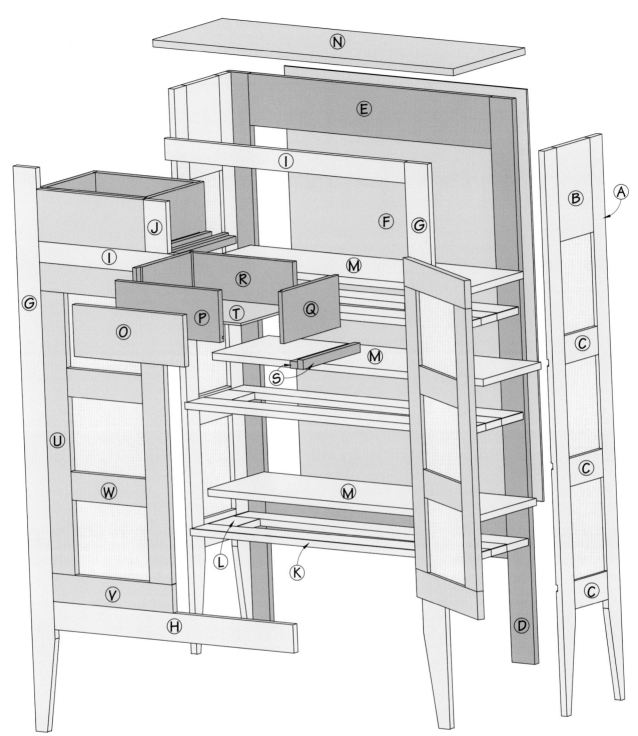

baked pies, tarts and breads to escape; the screens or panels also added to the aesthetics of the piece. Smaller versions with screens of a much finer mesh were used as milk safes. These pie safes were a part of most kitchens well into the middle of the twentieth century and, with the resurgence of country decor, are enjoying a new popularity.

You'll find cheaply constructed versions in most country craft stores and at the larger outdoor craft shows. These are poorly constructed pieces, air-nailed and glued together, finished only with a dark or simulated aged-pine stain; they usually sell anywhere from $125 to $200, depending upon the size; you get what you pay for.

I've seen better, factory-constructed pieces in some of the larger furniture stores. Most are made of oak, fitted with punched tin panels (obviously done by a machine), with a natural finish and a high gloss: not in the least authentic. They sell for between $500 and $800.

WHAT'S IT WORTH?

It should sell wholesale for around $350 and to order for at least $550. The cost of materials is less than $70.

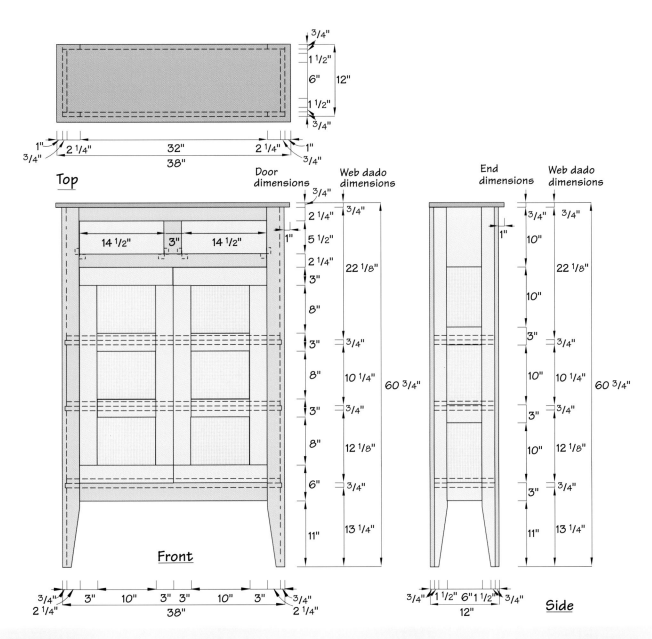

MATERIALS LIST

Pie Safe

No.	Letter	Item	Dimensions T W L	No.	Letter	Item	Dimensions T W L
4	A	Sides	¾″ × 2½″ × 60″	6	M	Web Frames	¾″ × 5½″ × 6″
2	B	Sides	¾″ × 6″ × 10″	3	N	Shelves	¾″ × 11″ × 37″
6	C	Sides	¾″ × 3″ × 6″	1	O	Top	¾″ × 13″ × 40″
1	D	Sides	¼″ × 6½″ × 10½″	4	P	Drawer Fronts	¾″ × 5½″ × 14½″
2	E	Back	¾″ × 3″ × 60″	4	Q	Drawer Sides	¾″ × 5½″ × 11¾″
2	F	Back	¾″ × 5″ × 32″	4	R	Drawer Backs	¾″ × 5″ × 14″
1	G	Back	¾″ × 30⅜″ × 39″	4	S	Drawer Guides	¾″ × 1″ × 11¾″
2	H	Front	¾″ × 3″ × 60″	4	T	Drawer Bottoms	¾″ × 13″ × 11¾″
2	I	Front	¾″ × 3″ × 32″	4	U	Door Stiles	¾″ × 3″ × 29½″
1	J	Front	¾″ × 2½″ × 32″	4	V	Door Rails	¾″ × 3″ × 16″
1	K	Front	¾″ × 3″ × 5″	4	W	Door Rails	¾″ × 3″ × 10″
4	L	Web Frames	¾″ × 2½″ × 37″				

CONSTRUCTION OUTLINE

The pie safe described on the following pages is an heirloom piece, constructed mostly with rails and stiles, floating panels, chicken wire screens and hand-cut swivel catches for an authentic, early 1800s look. The drawers are constructed just as they would have been in such a utility piece a couple of hundred years ago using lap joints, glue and nails. Dovetails might have been used, but rarely. The piece is finished using a ten-step painting process to make it look at least 150 years old.

It took some twenty hours, including finishing, over a two-week period to make, so you could easily complete the construction over a couple of long weekends; the finishing will take at least another week.

BUILDING THE PIE SAFE

STEP 1. Cut all the pieces for the side, back and front frames, web frames and all three shelves. Leave the door frames and drawers until later.

STEP 2. Set your table saw for grooving: the blade to a cutting depth of ¼″ and rip fence ¼″ away from the blade.

STEP 3. Groove all the pieces as described below. Cut one way, then reverse the piece and cut again; this will give you a ¼″ groove properly centered.

STEP 4. Lay out the sides as per the drawing using two pieces 60″×2½″, one 10″×6″, three pieces 6″×3″ and mark for biscuits. Be sure to number each joint.

STEP 5. Maintaining the layout, mill the biscuit slots then dry fit all of the pieces together, including three pieces of 10½″×6½″ lauan. Make any necessary adjustments, then glue up and clamp. Set aside and leave overnight to cure.

STEP 6. Lay out the back and construct as in steps 4 and 5.

STEP 7. Lay out the front frame as in step 4. Join the top rail (32″×3″), lower top rail (32″×2½″) and the drawer divider (5½″×3″) first, then proceed to assemble the result along with the rest of the front frame as in step 6.

STEP 8. At this point sand the faces of all the frames. This will make life much easier later on.

STEP 9. Lay out and construct the two web frames as in steps 4 and 5, then sand.

STEP 10. Dado both of the two side frames (one left, one right) as per the following: rabbet the inside top edges to a depth of ¼″ to take one of the web frames. Dado for the drawer support web frame 8⅞″ from the top of each piece to the bottom of the dado. The bottom of each of the other three dadoes is 13″ from the bottom of the one preceding. This gives a clearance between each shelf of 12¼″.

STEP 11. Sand and stain the shelves. Stain the inner surfaces of sides and front frame and both sides of the back with Puritan Pine; don't forget to do the end grain and edges.

STEP 12. Build the carcass—sides, shelves and web frames—glue, fit and toenail each shelf on the underside and clamp, then set aside and leave overnight to cure.

Note: If you intend to finish the piece as I have done, you can assemble the front and back frames to the carcass using glue, screws and plugs; all will be covered with several coats of paint—you can skip steps 13 through 15 and move on to step 16.

STEP 13. Attach the back to the carcass with clamps and mark for biscuits.

STEP 14. Mark the front frame and carcass as in step 13.

STEP 15. Mill biscuit slots.

STEP 16. Glue up and attach front and back frames to the carcass, clamp and leave overnight to cure.

STEP 17. Cut, stain and fit drawer guides.

STEP 18. If you haven't already done so, cut the pieces for the top, glue up, clamp and, when cured, round the edges of the front and ends.

STEP 19. Sand, stain and fit the top.

STEP 20. Measure the door opening and cut the door rails and stiles, making any adjustments needed for a snug fit.

STEP 21. Lay out the door frames and mark for biscuits (see drawing for configuration—note this layout makes for a strong door).

STEP 22. Mill the biscuit slots, glue and clamp the doors, making sure they are flat and square, then set aside for twenty-four hours to cure.

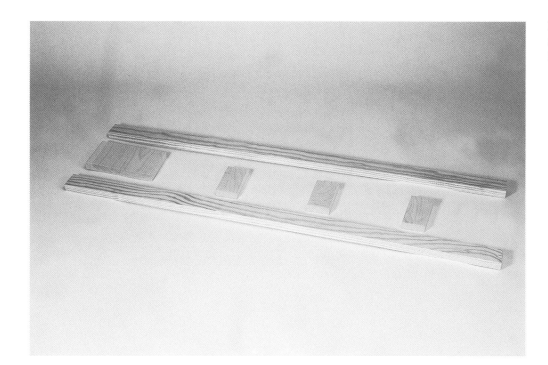

Lay out the sides of the pie safe and mark the pieces for biscuit slots.

STEP 23. When the glue has fully cured, rabbet ¼″ × ¼″ the inside edges of the three open panels in each of the two door frames.

STEP 24. Sand and stain the door frames.

STEP 25. Measure the drawer openings and cut the pieces for the drawers as set out in the materials list, making any adjustments for a snug fit. Sand carefully and stain.

STEP 26. Rabbet the inside edges of the drawer fronts leaving ¼″ of material on the outer face.

STEP 27. Rabbet the drawer sides on one end leaving ¼″ of material on the outer face.

STEP 28. Using one of the drawer backs as a template, set the table saw rip fence to 5″ and the blade to cut at a depth of ¼″. Cut slots in the sides and front of both drawers to accept a ¼″ plywood bottom: cut once then move the rip fence *out* to 5⅛″ and cut again. Be sure you make two left- and two right-hand sides.

STEP 29. Assemble the drawers using glue and cut-steel nails, then clamp and set them aside until the glue is fully cured.

STEP 30. Fit the drawer bottoms and secure them in place with a couple of brads to the back edges.

STEP 31. Attach two knobs, one to each drawer front.

STEP 32. Fit the doors to the carcass, measure and mark for butt hinges and cut mortises. Attach the doors to make sure everything fits and then remove them

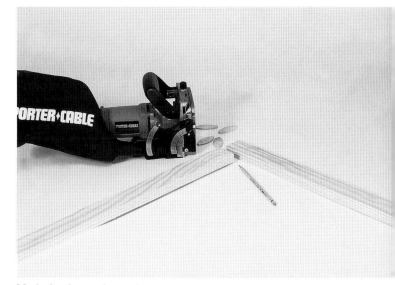

Mark the door stiles and rails for biscuits and cut the slots.

again—trim the doors if necessary. Attach the knobs and set aside for finishing.

STEP 33. Cut the metal blanks for the punched tin panels to size so they will fit the rabbets in the door frames.

STEP 34. Using the layout provided and a sharpened nail set, punch out the pattern on all six pieces of tin.

STEP 35. Using small strips of wood—beads—fasten the tin panels in place in the door frames.

At this point you should have most of the assembly complete and all of the pieces—the carcass, drawers and doors—should be stained Puritan pine. It's time to start the finishing process.

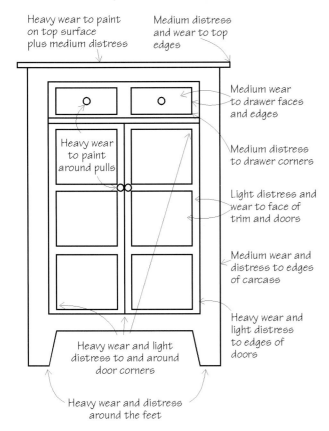

Heavy wear to paint on top surface plus medium distress

Medium distress and wear to top edges

Medium wear to drawer faces and edges

Heavy wear to paint around pulls

Medium distress to drawer corners

Light distress and wear to face of trim and doors

Medium wear and distress to edges of carcass

Heavy wear and light distress to edges of doors

Heavy wear and light distress to and around door corners

Heavy wear and distress around the feet

This diagram shows the typical areas of wear on most cabinets. Use the diagram as a guide to the location and extent of distressing on the pie safe.

FINISHING

The finish I've applied to this piece is designed to mimic one that might have built up over a great many years. As mentioned in the section on finishing, people of the eighteenth and nineteenth centuries liked bright colors—red, blue, green and white. Over the years they painted and repainted, especially kitchen furniture, many times. Wear, tear and distress would then reveal most of the layers. The following is a ten-step program that, if followed properly, will make your pie safe look at least 150 years old.

Aging With Paint Layers

STEP 1. Gently sand all of the outer surfaces with 220-grit paper, taking care not to remove any of the stain.

STEP 2. Distress. If you've never done this before you'll find it traumatic at first. It takes no little willpower to take up a rock and beat the heck out of a finely crafted piece, but the result, if not overdone, can be very pleasing. Use the drawing to identify the spots that need distressing.

STEP 3. Coat all outer surfaces with water-based, semi-gloss polyurethane and allow twenty-four hours to cure. This is to protect the stain during subsequent steps.

STEP 4. Paint all outer surfaces with bright red latex enamel. *Do not fill in the distress marks*—go over them lightly. Allow the paint to cure for at least twenty-four hours. What you now have is a pie safe from hell, but don't worry, things can only get better.

STEP 5. Apply diluted liquid hide glue (see chapter three, "Finishing") in random areas to the outer surfaces—the carcass, doors and drawers—feathering it out from heavy to very light (don't overdo it), and allow to cure overnight.

STEP 6. Working quickly, paint the entire outer surface with a dark green satin or semigloss paint. I used a hunter green specially mixed for me—you should go with a green you like. Allow the paint to cure completely. As it cures, you'll notice the areas where you applied the hide glue will begin to crackle.

STEP 7. Using 400-grit wet-and-dry sandpaper, gently rub the painted surfaces. Do not use water. If you do, you'll cause a new reaction from the hide glue that will destroy the finish. Instead, use paint thinner to lubricate the wet-and-dry paper. In places you'll want to go right through the green paint to show the red and even beyond to the stain below, which will look just like old, weathered pine—very nice. Pay attention to the crackled areas. Rub these only enough to remove the ridges and show the red paint below, no more. They should look something like rivers on a map.

STEP 8. Apply a coat of oil-based satin polyurethane to all painted surfaces. Allow to cure overnight, then rub over with 0000-gauge steel wool.

STEP 9. Apply a coat of dark antiquing glaze (see chapter three) to all painted surfaces, wiping most of it off as you go. This will give the piece a somewhat dingy look, darken the distressing marks and age the piece significantly. The glaze will dry quickly, and you can move on to the final step almost immediately.

STEP 10. Finally, apply one or two coats of oil-based satin polyurethane, sanding very gently between coats for a smooth finish.

Chapter 17

Eighteenth-Century Chimney Cabinet

These pieces were made to fit nicely beside a fire-place mantle. Some were little more than 12″ wide while some were a couple of feet or more.

Today they make great conversation pieces, interesting projects and they sell well. This version is a copy of one made around the turn of the nineteenth century.

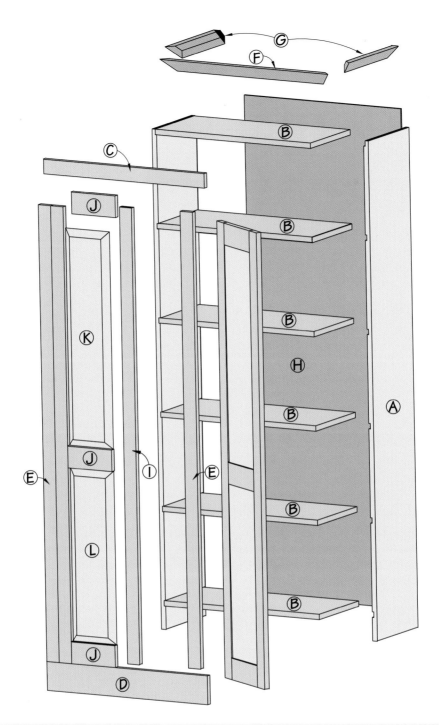

MATERIALS LIST

Chimney Cabinet

No.	Letter	Item	Dimensions T W L
2	A	Sides	¾″ × 11¼″ × 69″
6	B	Shelves, Bottom and Top	¾″ × 11¼″ × 23″
1	C	Trim Top	¾″ × 2″ × 24″
1	D	Trim Bottom	¾″ × 4″ × 24″
2	E	Trim Uprights	¾″ × 2″ × 63″
1	F	*Crown	¾″ × 2½″ × 27″

No.	Letter	Item	Dimensions T W L
2	G	*Crown	¾″ × 2½″ × 14″
2	H	Back	¼″ × 24″ × 69″
4	I	Door Stiles	¾″ × 2″ × 69″
6	J	Door Rails	¾″ × 3″ × 7″
2	K	Door Panels	¾″ × 7½″ × 30½″
2	L	Door Panels	¾″ × 7½″ × 24½″

*allows for trimming

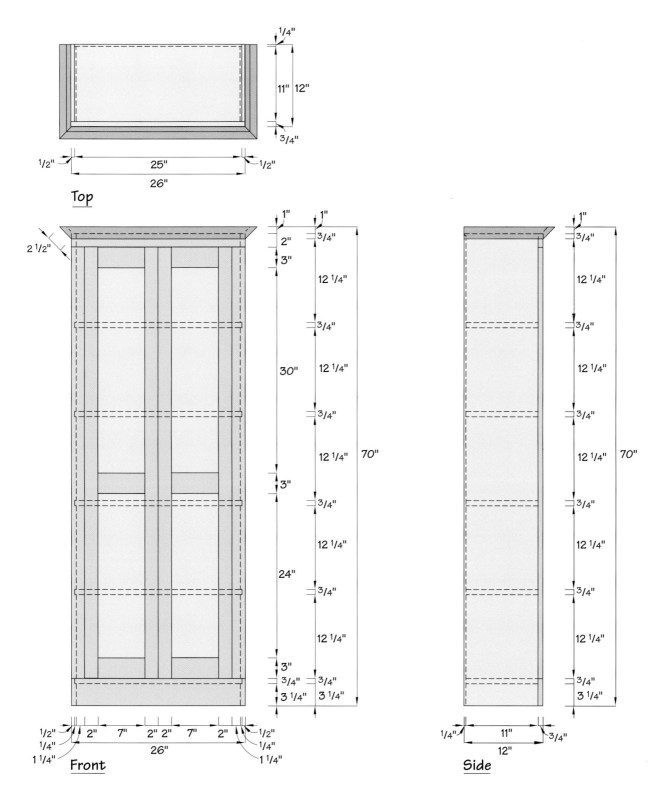

Top

Front

Side

WHAT'S IT WORTH?

An original in good condition might sell for $1,500 to $2,000. Surprisingly, a good copy can fetch almost as much. I've seen mine retail for as much as $950. Again, it depends on the quality, finish and location.

CONSTRUCTION OUTLINE

This is a simple project. With the exception of the raised-panel doors, construction is quite straightforward and shouldn't take more than a couple of weekends.

The sides are made from single pieces of stock, dadoed to take the six shelves, including top and bottom.

When making the doors, you can fasten the rails and stiles together with lap joints or biscuits. As you can see, I prefer to use biscuits. It's quick, simple and strong.

These can be set equidistant apart, or you can vary them to allow room to store larger objects at the bottom and smaller ones at the top. The trim can be fastened to the carcass with glue and nails or with biscuits and glue. The crown is constructed from three pieces of stock, the edges beveled to 45°, the ends mitered then glued and screwed to the top. The back is made from a single piece of lauan plywood, but you could go the distance and use ½″ tongue-and-grooved boards, as you would likely find on an original piece. The two doors are constructed with raised panels and secured to the carcass with reproduction "H" hinges, stripped and aged for authenticity. For the finish I chose dark blue paint over white and a dark stain.

BUILDING THE CABINET

STEP 1. Cut all the pieces to size.

STEP 2. Mill the dadoes to the two sides as laid out in the drawing.

STEP 3. Sand both faces of the sides smooth and apply your chosen stain—it's much easier to do this now than when assembly is complete.

STEP 4. Sand both surfaces of all four shelves, bottom and top, and then apply your stain.

STEP 5. Using glue, clamps and toenails, assemble the carcass. Check the diagonals to make sure the structure is square, then set it aside until the glue is fully cured.

To mill the grooves in the edges of the rails and stiles that will house the door panels, you can use your router table and a ⁵⁄₁₆″ bit, or your table saw. I run a piece of table along the top of the back fence and, to ensure the groove is consistently in the proper place, mark the start and stop points as you see here.

STEP 6. Sand the trim smooth and apply stain.

STEP 7. Once the clamps are removed, lay the carcass on its back, set the trim in place and mark for biscuit slots. It's best if you allow 8″ or 9″ between biscuits.

STEP 8. Mill the biscuit slots.

STEP 9. Glue and clamp the trim in place and set the structure aside until the glue is fully cured.

The door panels are quite small and easily handled on the table saw. Set the angle of the blade to between 15° and 17°, and then set the depth of cut so that the tip of the blade just breaks through the surface of the panel.

To make the crown, trim the edges of all three pieces of stock to 45°. Do this so that both angles are on the same side so that, when you look at the end grain, you see a triangle with a flat top.

STEP 10. Use either your router with a ⁵⁄₁₆″ straight-cutting bit or your table saw to mill ⅜″-deep grooves to the inner edges of the rails and stiles that will make up the doors.

STEP 11. Lay out the rails and stiles and mark for biscuit slots. You can use lap joints if you like, but you'll need to adjust the length of the rails to maintain the outer dimensions of the doors.

STEP 12. Mill the biscuit slots.

STEP 13. Dry fit the rails and stiles and measure the width

and height between the grooves to ensure the panels will fit properly.

STEP 14. If necessary, trim the panels to size.

STEP 15. Sand the rails and stiles smooth and apply your stain.

STEP 16. Glue and clamp the rails and stiles, *one side only*, dry fit the other and set them aside until the glue is fully cured.

STEP 17. Set your table saw to cut at an angle of 17°, the

To form the miters on the ends of the crown, set the miter gauge to 45°, place one of the mitered edges against the face of the miter gauge and the other down on the saw table, and then gently make the cut.

rip fence at ¼″, and mill the bevels to the edges of the panels.

STEP 18. Sand the panels smooth, paying close attention to the bevels, then apply the stain.

STEP 19. When the glue is fully cured, remove the clamps from the frames and remove the dry-fitted stiles.

STEP 20. Slide the panels into place in the now-open frames, glue and clamp the remaining stiles in place, and set the completed doors aside to allow the glue to fully cure.

STEP 21. Use a beading bit in your router table to detail the edges of the three pieces of stock that will make the crown, then cut the miters.

STEP 22. Set the crown in place on the carcass, check for size, make any necessary adjustments then glue and screw the pieces in place.

STEP 23. Set the doors in place and make any necessary adjustments for a good fit.

STEP 24. You've now reached the point where you'll need to complete the finishing process (see right).

STEP 25. When finishing is complete, set the doors in place and attach the hinges and knobs; the project is complete.

FINISHING

If you've done your staining as you worked your way through the project, all that now remains to complete the finish is to do some light distressing around the trim, the corners and edges of the doors, a little final sanding with a fine-grit paper and then add the paint. The choice between colors, one over the other, is a personal one; I used dark blue over white. Finally, to complete the illusion, you'll need to apply some sort of antiquing glaze. I recommend you use the polyurethane-pigment combination described in chapter three.

Chapter 18

Bachelor's Chest/ Linen Press

This bachelor's chest was a prized piece of furniture during the eighteenth century and has remained so. The design, a linen press over a chest of drawers, is English and was imported to America more than 200 years ago. It's a large, functional and attractive piece. The one I have chosen is a copy of one made in Connecticut circa 1830. You can make it with three shelves in the press section, or you can leave two

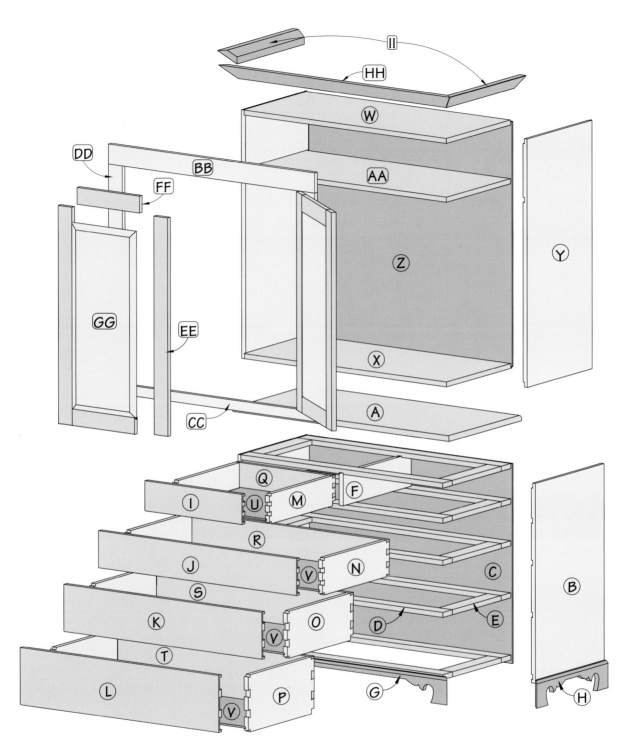

of them out and use the piece as an entertainment center; the top shelf will nicely accommodate a VCR and the large opening a 19″ television.

WHAT'S IT WORTH?

If you were to buy a modern version of this piece it would cost you at least $1,200, perhaps as much as $2,000. An original, if you could find one, might go for as much as $9,000.

CONSTRUCTION OUTLINE

The piece is made in two parts, and for the sake of mobility and convenience, the parts should remain separate, the upper section freestanding on the lower section. For such a seemingly complicated piece, construction is relatively simple with a couple of exceptions.

The original was made from walnut. I don't think pine was ever used. Still, there's no reason why it shouldn't be used. I decided to use furniture grade throughout.

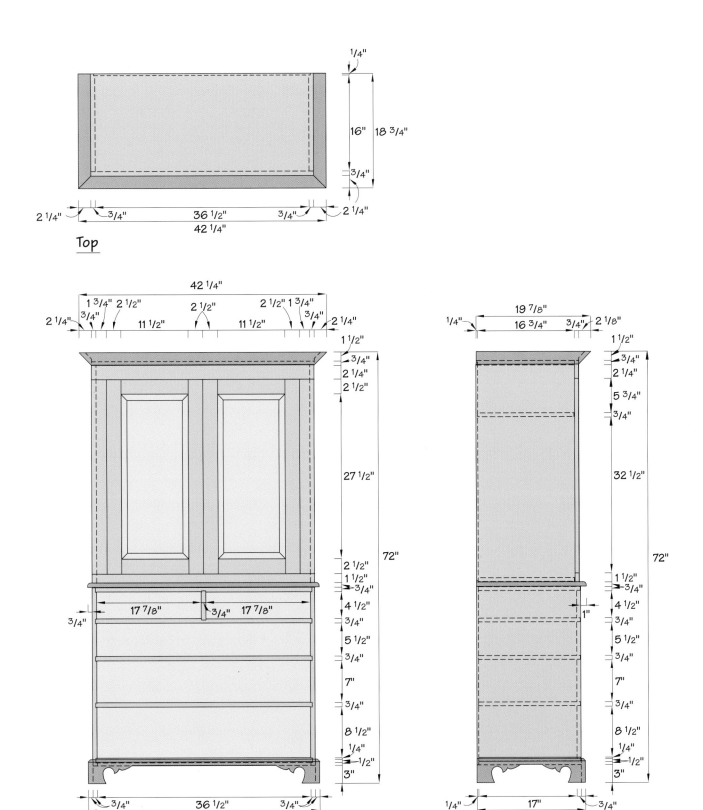

Top

Front

Side

It's stable, predictable, easy to work and takes stain well.

The upper section, the press, is no more than a cupboard with a single shelf (three, if you decide not to make it as an entertainment center). The shelves are dadoed into its sides; the top and bottom are rabbeted into the sides; the plywood back is also set into rabbets. The trim is fastened to the front with biscuits and glue, and the crown is fastened to the top with glue and screws. The hardware consists of reproduction brass knobs and "H" hinges.

Bachelors Chest

No.	Letter	Item	Dimensions T W L
Drawer Section			
1	A	Top	¾" × 19" × 39½"
2	B	Case Sides	¾" × 18" × 29¾"
1	C	Case Back	¼" × 29¾" × 37½"
10	D	Web Parts	¾" × 2½" × 37"
10	E	Web Parts	¾" × 4" × 12¾"
1	F	Drawer Partition	¾" × 4½" × 17¾"
1	G	*Foot	¾" × 4" × 42"
2	H	*Feet	¾" × 4" × 22"
2	I	Drawer Fronts	¾" × 4½" × 17⅝"
1	J	Drawer Front	¾" × 5½" × 36½"
1	K	Drawer Front	¾" × 7" × 36½"
1	L	Drawer Front	¾" × 8½" × 36½"
4	M	Drawer Sides	¾" × 4½" × 17½"
2	N	Drawer Sides	¾" × 5½" × 17½"
2	O	Drawer Sides	¾" × 7" × 17½"
2	P	Drawer Sides	¾" × 8½" × 17½"
2	Q	Drawer Backs	¾" × 4" × 17⅝"
1	R	Drawer Back	¾" × 5" × 17⅝"
1	S	Drawer Back	¾" × 6½" × 17⅝"
1	T	Drawer Back	¾" × 8" × 17⅝"
2	U	Drawer Bottoms	¾" × 16⅝" × 17½"
3	V	Drawer Bottoms	¾" × 35½" × 17½"
Press Section			
1	W	Top	¾" × 17" × 37"
1	X	Bottom	¾" × 17" × 37"
2	Y	Sides	¾" × 17" × 37"
1	Z	Back	¼" × 37½" × 36½"
1	AA	Shelf	¾" × 16½" × 37"
1	BB	Trim	¾" × 3" × 38"
1	CC	Trim	¾" × 1½" × 38"
2	DD	Trim	¾" × 2½" × 32½"
4	EE	Door Stiles	¾" × 2½" × 32½"
4	FF	Door Rails	¾" × 3" × 11½"
2	GG	Door Panels	¾" × 12" × 28"
1	HH	*Crown	¾" × 3" × 43"
2	II	*Crown	¾" × 3" × 20"

*Extra length added for cutting

The bottom section is no more than a simple chest of drawers with web frames dadoed into the sides. The top is a board constructed from several smaller pieces of stock; the grains are alternated for stability. The feet are cut from single pieces of stock. The drawers are constructed using half-blind and through dovetails.

BUILDING THE DRAWER SECTION

STEP 1. Cut all the pieces to size and run the edges through the jointer.

STEP 2. Build the boards that will make the sides, top and bottom.

STEP 3. Build the four web frames as laid out in the drawing—you can use biscuits, as I did, or lap joints. Note the offsets, and also the frame, which has an extra stretcher to carry the separator that will support the drawers.

STEP 4. Mark the sides for stopped dadoes and top and bottom stopped rabbets as laid out in the drawing.

STEP 5. Mill the stopped dadoes and rabbets. I used my router, a ¾" mortising bit and a T-square jig as described in the Shop Tip on page 123.

STEP 6. Mill ¼"-deep rabbets to the inside back edges of both sides; these will receive the plywood back.

When sanding the butt joints on the side section, or any butt joints, use your belt sander and work first across the joint and grain in a diagonal direction, and then finish with the belt sander by working the machine along the direction of the grain.

Finish sanding with your random orbital sander, making sure to remove all the tool and belt marks, especially on the knots.

STEP 7. Glue, clamp and toenail the webs and bottom board to the sides; make sure everything is square, and then set the structure aside until the glue is fully cured.

STEP 8. Glue and screw the drawer separator in place between the top and the top web frame as laid out in the drawing.

STEP 9. Set the top board in place on the top web frame and fasten it in place using ten no. $6 \times 1\frac{5}{8}''$ screws: four at the back and front, and one at each end.

STEP 10. Use the scale pattern to mark the feet details.

STEP 11. Cut the miters to each end of the four pieces of stock that will make the feet.

STEP 12. Use either your band saw or jigsaw to cut out the feet.

STEP 13. From the inside, glue and screw the feet to the bottom of the carcass, making sure they are level and true.

STEP 14. Make sure all the pieces for all five drawers are exactly the right size, then using half-blind and through dovetail joints, build the drawers. You can see how in the Shop Tip on page 98.

BUILDING THE PRESS SECTION

STEP 15. Build the boards that will make the sides, shelf (or shelves), top and bottom.

STEP 16. Mark the sides for dadoes and top and bottom rabbets as laid out in the drawing.

STEP 17. Mill the dadoes and rabbets.

STEP 18. Mill $\frac{1}{4}''$-deep rabbets to the inside back edges of both sides to receive the plywood back.

STEP 19. Glue, clamp and toenail the shelf (or shelves), top and bottom to the sides; make sure everything is square, then set the structure aside until the glue is fully cured.

STEP 20. Lay the carcass flat on its back on the bench, put the trim in place and mark for biscuit slots. If you don't use biscuits you can glue, clamp and nail the pieces in place.

STEP 21. Remove the trim and mill the biscuit slots.

Use your table saw or router table to mill the groove along the front and sides of the drawer sections.

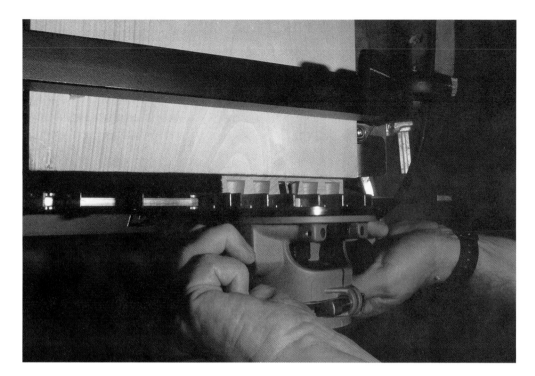

Milling blind dovetail joints is a simple job if you have a dovetail jig. It just takes attention to detail and an effort to make sure the stock is properly placed in the jig, touching all the stops and fingers. Just a small deviation will produce a sloppy joint.

There's nothing quite so satisfying as the perfectly finished joint.

STEP 22. Glue and clamp the trim in place. If you've used nails, now's the time to set the heads and fill the holes.

STEP 23. Build the two doors as laid out in the drawing and the Shop Tip on page 91.

STEP 24. Set your table saw to cut at an angle of 45° and a depth of 1¼″ and cut the bevels to the three pieces of stock that will make the lower section of the crown.

STEP 25. Cut the miters to the ends of the crown.

STEP 26. Use a ½″ roundover bit in your router to round the front edges of the three pieces that will make the upper section of the crown.

STEP 27. Glue the miters, set the upper section of the crown in place and secure to the top of the carcass using nine no. 6 × 1⅝″ screws: four along the front and three at each end.

STEP 28. Apply glue to the edges and miters of the three pieces of the lower section of the crown, set them in place, then secure them with a couple of brads.

STEP 29. Use small brads to attach the plywood back to the back of the unit.

STEP 30. Apply a coat of stain to both sections, chest and press, then move on to the finishing process.

STEP 31. After finishing is complete you can attach the knobs to the doors, the pulls to the drawers, and then fit the doors to the cupboard section using reproduction hinges.

FINISHING

How to finish a nice piece such as this is a tough decision. I decided to keep things relatively simple. Thinking that it would be used in a bedroom and therefore would not be subject to heavy traffic and wear and tear, I decided to go with a little light distressing—just a ding or two, here and there—a very dark stain (I used Jacobean by Minwax) and a couple of coats of shellac. Finally, I finished the process with a couple of coats of beeswax buffed to a shine.

SHOP TIP
Cutting Dados With a Router

You can cut dados a number of ways: on the table saw, on a radial arm saw, or you can do as I do and use your router.

Over the years, I've found the router to be the best, most reliable and most convenient way to cut dados. You'll find it very convenient not having to break down your table saw or radial arm to fit the stacked dodo head. You'll also find the finished product is much better. The bottom of a dado cut with a router is dead square and flat, and the two sections will fit tightly and squarely together, making final squaring of the piece extremely simple.

To mill dados with a router, you'll need a couple things. First, obviously, you'll need an appropriate bit: ¾″ × 1″ if you're using standard stock—one with carbide tips works best.

Next, you'll need a jig. I use a simple, home-made T square. Make the T long enough so the router will pass through it the first time you use it. This makes setting the square for future cuts extremely simple.

Finally, you'll need a clamp to hold the square in place while you make the cut. I love the little, quick-release clamp you see in the photo. It's made by Bessy, and makes setting and re-setting the square quick and easy.

Finally, set the depth of cut on your router to ¼″, or whatever depth you prefer, clamp the square in place and make the cut.

I've cut thousands upon thousands of dados, in stock of widths from 3″ or 4″ to as much as 3′ or even more, always with the very best results. I wouldn't even consider doing it any other way. Once you get used to it, it's very quick and easy to do.

Chapter 19

High Chest

The chest of drawers was the result of the natural evolution of the blanket chest. First came the "chest on drawers." First one drawer, then another and another were added to the simple blanket chest until, finally, by the turn of the eigthteenth-century, the box section had been done away with alto-gether, leaving the chest of drawers we know so well today. Mr. Chippendale's famous *Gentleman and Cabinet-Maker's Director* of 1774 shows several nice versions. The high chest I've chosen is a copy of one found in Charleston, South Carolina, circa 1790–1810.

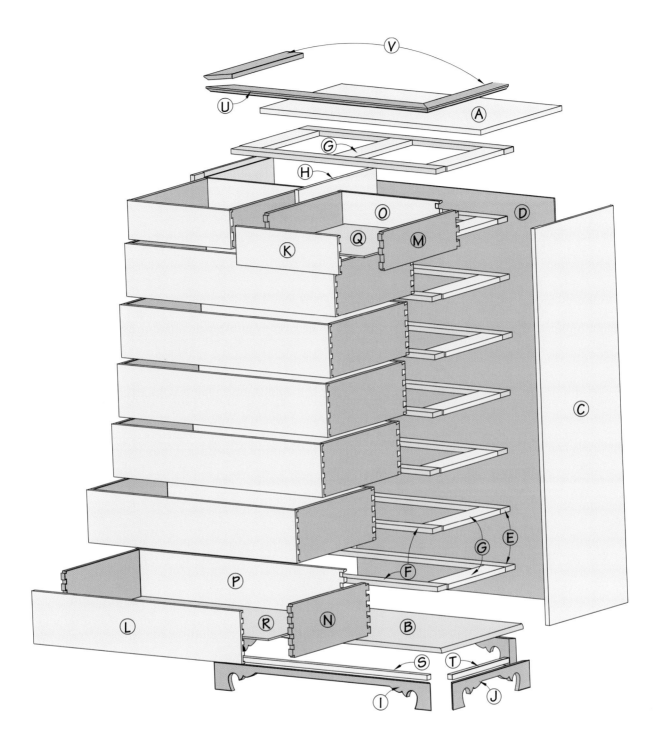

WHAT'S IT WORTH?

A chest such as this routinely sells in fine furniture stores for $800 and up. Depending upon the quality of the piece you should be able to ask at least $400 for this piece. It's quite unique and much in demand.

CONSTRUCTION OUTLINE

This is a substantial piece of furniture. It's bulky, heavy and difficult to maneuver. The carcass is of web frame construction with solid sides and top. The sides are stop-dadoed to receive the webs, and present a clean, unbroken front. The webs are offset for the same reason. The chest itself stands on feet attached to the bottom of the carcass. These are shaped, glued and then screwed in place from the underside of the one-piece bottom. The drawers are constructed using half-blind dovetail joints and fitted with period wooden knobs.

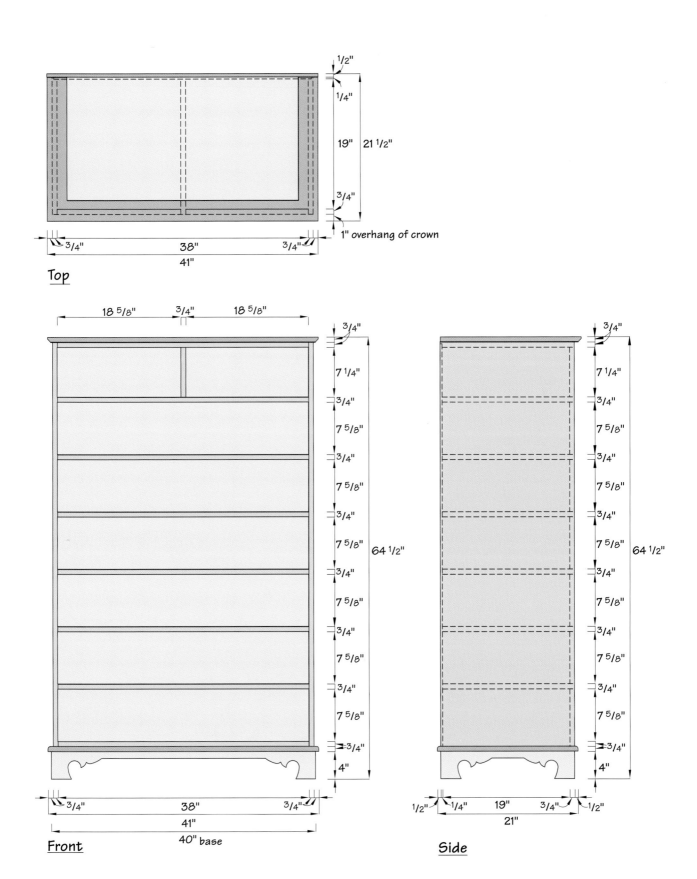

1/2"

1/4"

19"   21 1/2"

3/4"

1" overhang of crown

3/4"   38"   3/4"

41"

Top

18 5/8"   3/4"   18 5/8"

3/4"

7 1/4"

3/4"

7 5/8"

3/4"

7 5/8"

3/4"

7 5/8"

3/4"

7 5/8"

3/4"

7 5/8"

3/4"

7 5/8"

3/4"

4"

64 1/2"

3/4"   38"   3/4"

41"

40" base

Front

3/4"

7 1/4"

3/4"

7 5/8"

3/4"

7 5/8"

3/4"

7 5/8"

3/4"

7 5/8"

3/4"

7 5/8"

3/4"

7 5/8"

3/4"

4"

64 1/2"

1/2"   1/4"   19"   3/4"   1/2"

21"

Side

BUILDING THE CHEST

STEP 1. Cut all the pieces to size and run the edges through the jointer.

STEP 2. Build the boards that will make the sides, top and bottom.

STEP 3. Build the seven web frames (including one at the bottom to which the bottom board will be attached) as laid out in the drawing. You can use biscuits, as I did, or lap joints. Note the offsets, and that the top frame has an extra stretcher to carry the drawer separator.

STEP 4. Mark the sides for stopped dadoes and top and bottom stopped rabbets as laid out in the drawing.

MATERIALS LIST

High Chest

No.	Letter	Item	Dimensions T W L
1	A	Top	¾" × 21" × 41"
1	B	Bottom	¾" × 21" × 41"
2	C	Sides	¾" × 20" × 59"
1	D	*Back	¾" × 39½" × 60"
8	E	Webs	¾" × 2½" × 38½"
8	F	Webs	¾" × 2½" × 38"
18	G	Webs	¾" × 4" × 14¾"
1	H	Drawer Separator	¾" × 5½" × 19¾"
2	I	Feet	¾" × 4" × 41"
2	J	Feet	¾" × 4" × 20"
2	K	Drawer Fronts	¾" × 5½" × 18⅞"
2	L	Drawer Fronts	¾" × 7⅞" × 38½"
2	M	Drawer Sides	¾" × 5½" × 19¾"
2	N	Drawer Sides	¾" × 7⅞" × 19¾"
2	O	Drawer Backs	¾" × 5" × 19⅞"
2	P	Drawer Backs	¾" × 7⅜" × 38½"
2	Q	Drawer Bottoms	¼" × 18½" × 19½"
2	R	Drawer Bottoms	¼" × 38" × 19½"

*Overlaps slightly at the bottom

When you edge-join the pieces that make up the sides, mill your biscuit slots about 9" apart.

Cut the miters to the ends of the feet before you cut out the shapes.

Use your router with a ¾" bit and a T square to mill the stopped dadoes that will receive the top, bottom and web frames.

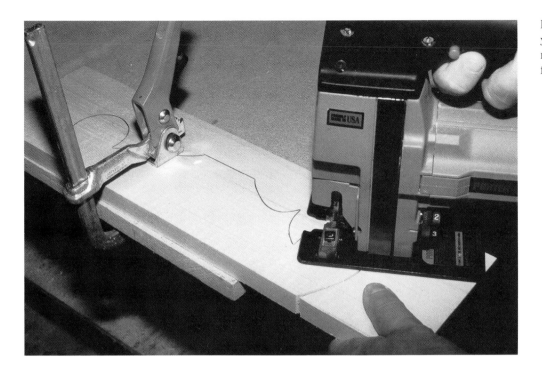

If you don't have a scroll saw, your jigsaw is the best tool for removing the waste from the feet sections.

Bessy's block and clamp system makes gluing and clamping mitered frames easy.

STEP 5. Mill the stopped dadoes and rabbets. I used my router, a ¾″ mortising bit and a T-square jig as described in the Shop Tip on page 123.

STEP 6. Mill ¼″-deep rabbets to the inside back edges of both sides; these will receive the plywood back.

STEP 7. Glue, clamp and toenail the webs to the sides, making sure everything is square, and then set the structure aside until the glue is fully cured.

STEP 8. Glue and screw the drawer separator in place between the top and the top web frame as laid out in the drawing.

STEP 9. Set the carcass on the bottom board and fasten it in place using ten no. 6 × 1⅝″ screws: four at the back and front and one at each end. Be sure the heads do not protrude.

STEP 10. Use the scale pattern to mark the feet details.

STEP 11. Cut the miters to each end of the four pieces of stock that will make the feet.

Use a T square and your router equipped with a ¾" mortising bit to mill the stopped dadoes in the sides.

STEP 12. Use your band saw or jigsaw to cut out the feet.

STEP 13. Glue and clamp the feet section together to form a frame, make sure the structure is square, then set it aside until the glue is fully cured.

STEP 14. Glue and screw the cleats to the upper inside edge of the feet section.

STEP 15. Turn the carcass upside down, set the feet section in place on the bottom board and then using ten no. 6 × 1⅝" screws—four at the back and front and one at each end—attach it to the bottom board of the carcass.

STEP 16. Set your table saw to cut at an angle of 17° and a depth of 1¼" and cut the bevel to the three pieces of stock that will make the crown.

STEP 17. Cut the miters to the ends of the crown.

STEP 18. Glue the miters, set the crown in place and secure to the top of the carcass using ten no. 6 × 1⅝" screws: four along front and three at each end.

STEP 19. Make sure all the pieces for all eight drawers are exactly the right size, then, using half-blind and through dovetail joints, build the drawers (see the Shop Tip on page 98).

STEP 20. Use small brads to attach the plywood back to the back of the unit.

STEP 21. Do some final sanding, then go on to the finishing process.

This photo illustrates how to mark the front components of the web frames for biscuit slots. Note the offset.

FINISHING

I did very little distressing on this piece on the advice of a good friend who owns a very upscale furniture store. Just a ding or two here and there seemed to be all that was required. For the stain I used tobacco juice. I applied several coats, allowing each one to dry thoroughly before applying the next, until I had the deep, dark color I was looking for. Next, I applied eight coats of button-lac—it, too, has a dark color—sanding lightly between the coats. Finally, after a last wipe with 400-grit sandpaper, I applied two coats of beeswax and buffed to a shine.

Early Nineteenth-Century Harvest Table

The term harvest table usually designates a very long dining table with one or two drop leaves supported by swing-out or pullout brackets. They were made all over the United States, usually from pine, but many had a pine top and a hardwood under-structure. They were somewhat primitive in style, essentially unfinished as opposed to the highly polished dining room–style tables, and would have been found in homes of type and class. But most were country pieces, farmhouse furniture. Tables like this also would

have been used in kitchens, large and small, where the seating would have been benches rather than chairs. They came in all sizes from as small as 48″ long to as large as 10′. Ours is 54″ × 44″ when fully extended. I chose this size so it would fit comfortably even in a small dining area. You'll enjoy having a piece like this in your home just as much as you'll enjoy making it. The construction was quite simple, and the early versions might or might not have had a rule joint between the leaves; ours, a copy of one made around 1820, does not. Few

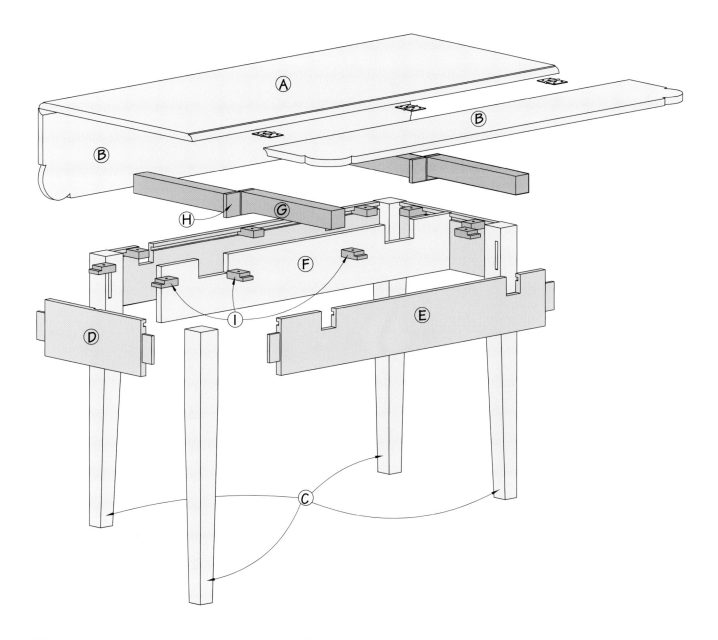

old harvest tables have survived the centuries. Those that have are well worn and in poor shape. So this one will make a rare conversation piece and will be sure to raise a few eyebrows.

WHAT'S IT WORTH

A reproduction table such as this, if you could find one, in a fine furniture store would fetch at least $600, perhaps as much as $800. An original would cost at least $2,500.

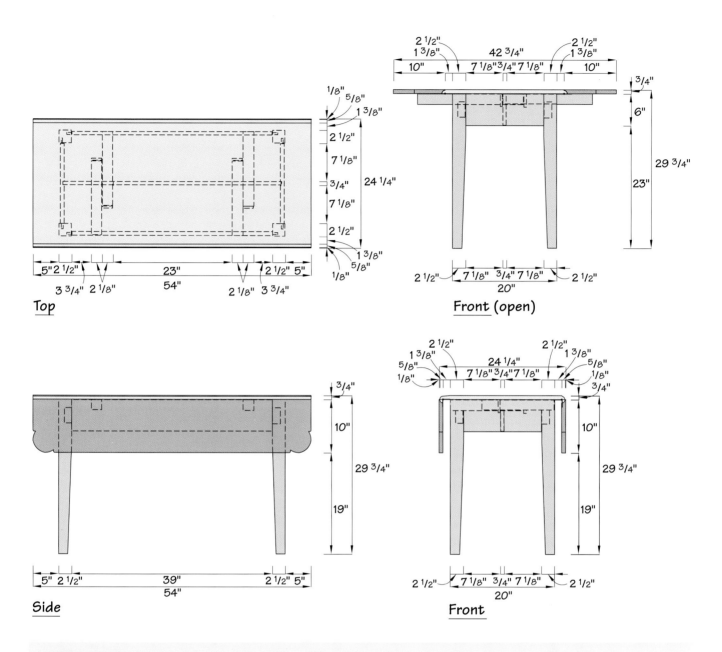

Top

Front (open)

Side

Front

MATERIALS LIST

Harvest Table

No.	Letter	Item	Dimensions T W L
1	A	Top	¾″ × 24″ × 54″
2	B	Leaves	¾″ × 10″ × 54″
4	C	Legs	2½″ × 2½″ × 29″
2	D	Short Aprons	¾″ × 6″ × 18″
2	E	Long Aprons	¾″ × 6″ × 42″

No.	Letter	Item	Dimensions T W L
1	F	Leaf Support Carrier	¾″ × 6″ × 42½″
4	G	Leaf Supports	2″ × 2″ × 14″
4	H	Stops	½″ × 2″ × 2½″
10	I	Buttons	¾″ × 1½″ × 2″

Note: There is a ¼″ setback on the aprons from the outside of the legs.

CONSTRUCTION OUTLINE

The top, 24″ wide, is made from three pieces of furniture-grade pine a full ¾″ thick, the grain alternated for stability. Each of the two leaves is made from a single piece of stock, also ¾″ wide, which will provide a tabletop 44″ wide when fully extended. The legs, made from 10/4 stock, are slightly tapered. The apron is mortised and tenoned to the legs. The leaf supports are simple pullouts set into cutaways in the apron. The top is fastened to the apron with a series of buttons placed strategically around the upper inside of the understructure. There are no drawers. You should be able to finish it over a couple of weekends.

BUILDING THE TABLE

STEP 1. Cut all the pieces to size and run the edges through the jointer to ensure they are straight and square.

STEP 2. Build the board that will become the tabletop. You can use biscuits, as I did, or the more traditional dowels. Be sure to alternate the grain for stability.

STEP 3. Use the scale pattern and your jigsaw to cut the details to the corners of the leaves.

STEP 4. Use a ½″ roundover bit in your router and round the upper edge of the ends of the top only, and the upper edge of the ends and outer edge of both leaves.

To begin working the detail at the ends of the leaves, on the underside at the outer edge of each end, scribe two lines 5″ from the corners in both directions.

A three-pound coffee can is just the right size to use for marking the circle. Join the ends of two short, then use your jigsaw to remove the waste.

Use a ½″ roundover bit to mill the outer edges of the two leaves and the ends of the tabletop.

Mark the position of the hinges on the underside of the top and leaves, score the outline with a utility knife, then remove the waste, freehand, with your router equipped with either a ¼″ or 5⁄16″ straight bit.

A tenoning jig makes short work of the joints at the ends of the apron, a sometimes tricky job. The results are consistent and accurate, but don't make the tenons until you've worked the mortises.

If your rip fence is movable, set it so that you can cut the shoulders of your tenons. If it's not movable, use a sacrifice fence attached to your rip fence.

STEP 5. Set your tapering jig to 2° and cut the tapers to the inside faces of all four legs. Leave the outside faces straight. Begin the taper 8″ from the top of the leg, and make sure you have two left- and two right-hand legs.

STEP 6. Cut mortises 3″ long × 1½″ deep × ⅜″ wide to the inside faces of all four legs, again making sure you have two left- and two right-hand legs.

STEP 7. Mill the matching tenons to all four pieces that will make up the apron.

STEP 8. Dry fit the pieces to ensure everything is as it should be, then disassemble the pieces.

STEP 9. Mill the ⅜″ slots to all four pieces of the apron that will receive the buttons to secure the top to the understructure.

STEP 10. Mill the dadoes in the inner faces of the two ends that will receive the leaf support carrier.

STEP 11. Mill the cutouts in the apron and carrier that will receive the leaf supports.

STEP 12. Sand all of the pieces smooth; do your distressing, to whatever degree suits you best, paying attention to the top, outer edges and corners, and to the bottom section of all four legs. Apply a coat of stain.

STEP 13. Glue, assemble and clamp the understructure—legs, apron and support carrier—and set aside overnight or until the glue is fully cured. I prefer to use one of the new polyurethane glues for this process.

Use your table saw equipped with a dado head to mill the button groove to the inner edge of the four rails that will make up the apron. If you don't have a dado head, you can use your regular blade, run the stock through once, and then move the rip fence and run it again.

STEP 14. Use no. $6 \times 1\frac{5}{8}$″ screws to fasten the stops to the ends of the pullout leaf supports.

STEP 15. Lay the top and leaves face down on the bench and mark the position of the mortises that will receive the hinges; use simple 3″ brass butt hinges.

STEP 16. Use your router and a ¼″ straight bit to mill the mortises, or you can use a chisel if that suits you best, then screw the hinges in place; leave the top face down on the bench.

STEP 17. Go to the band saw and make ten buttons from the $2″ \times 1\frac{1}{2}″ \times \frac{3}{4}″$ pieces of stock laid out in the materials list, as per the drawing.

STEP 18. Set the understructure in place on the underside of the top—it should still be on the bench—and slip the four pullout leaf supports into place.

STEP 19. Use four buttons along each side and one at each end to fasten the top in place on the understructure.

STEP 20. Go to the finishing process.

FINISHING

As this is supposed to be a simple farmhouse piece, finishing is minimal. An original, if not painted, would not have been finished at all. The pine would have been

For accuracy, you can use this setup on your band saw to cut the shoulders to the tenons of the rails that make up the apron. Set the rip fence in position, and then clamp your stop in position so that the blade of the saw just reaches the main body of the rail. If you don't have a rip fence, you can use a piece of scrap stock.

scrubbed and scrubbed over the years, would have suffered all sorts of abuse and would have taken on a deep, buttery yellow patina. So, as distressing is done purely to taste, I've only lightly distressed ours, and the finish is no more than a coat of Golden Pecan stain and a single wiping of antiquing glaze followed by a couple of coats of polyurethane for protection.

Chapter 21

Nineteenth-Century Dough Box

The dough box was a functional piece found in many a country kitchen. The idea was that the cook would make a large batch of bread dough, knead it on the large work surface that formed the lid, then throw it inside the box and leave it to rise. Once the dough had risen she would bring it out again, drop it once more on the surface of the lid and prepare it for the oven. Today, the piece is just as functional, though not used for dough. Most dough boxes are used as storage units, conversation pieces and decoration. They come in all shapes and sizes, depending upon the size of the house where they originated. Some had square

or tapered legs; others had turned legs. A large country home with a large family and staff would have required more baked goods than a small town house, thus the box would have been in the order of perhaps 48″ wide × 24″ deep × 27″ high. Ours is a smaller unit 36″ wide × 17″ deep × 27″ high. I found it in a book of American country antiques. It was dated to the early 1800s and was somewhat primitive in design. I have changed nothing except to add hinges to the one-time lift-off lid. This makes it a little more functional and convenient. What can you use it for? How about storing linens— tablecloths, napkins, etc.?

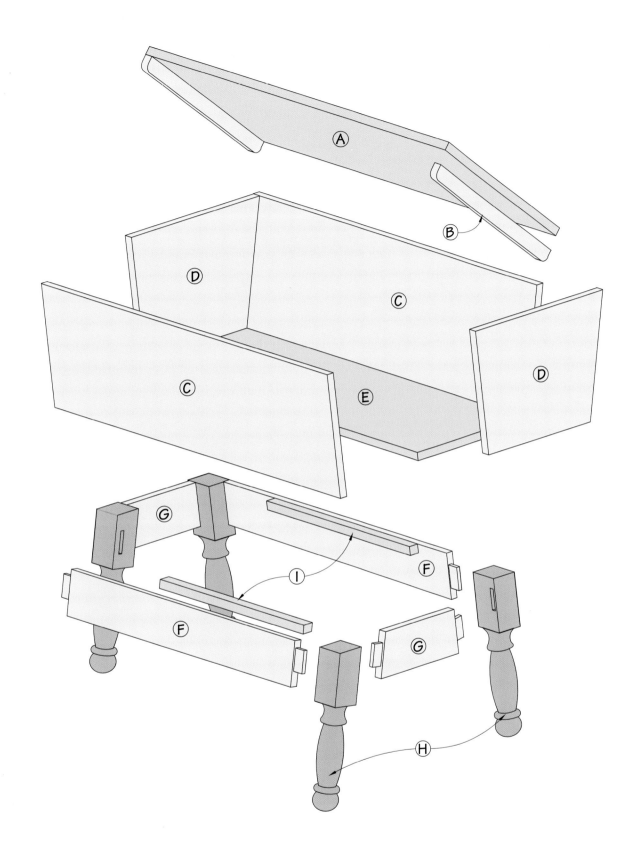

WHAT'S IT WORTH?

An original might fetch something in the region of $500 or $600. A reproduction, if well done, might fetch almost as much in a retail store; to the trade, perhaps $150–$200. Privately, depending upon your location, it would be worth $250 and up to whatever the market will bear.

CONSTRUCTION OUTLINE

For the sake of authenticity, I constructed the box section using glue and cut-steel nails. The ends are tapered to an angle of 8°. The bottom of the box is attached with screws. The top is a simple board built from several smaller pieces of stock, the grain alternated for stability,

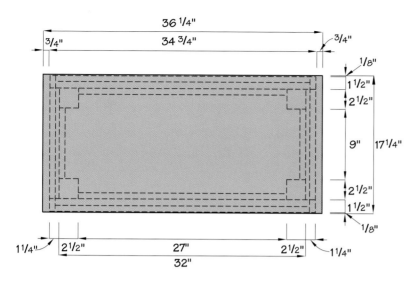

Top

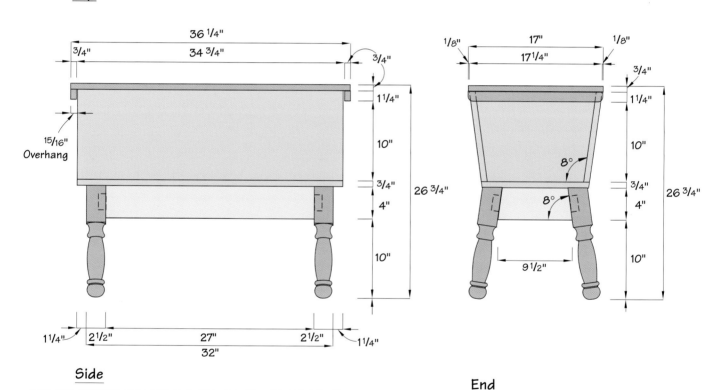

Side

End

MATERIALS LIST

Dough Box

No.	Letter	Item	Dimensions T W L
1	A	Top	¾″ × 36¼″ × 17″
2	B	Cleats	¾″ × 1¼″ × 17¼″
2	C	Box Sides	¾″ × 11¼″ × 34¼″
2	D	Box Ends	¾″ × 11¼″ × 15½″
1	E	Box Bottom	¾″ × 13¾″ × 34
2	F	Aprons	¾″ × 4″ × 29
2	G	Aprons	¾″ × 4″ × 10½″
4	H	Legs	2 ½″ × 2½″ × 14¼″

biscuited together. The original had cleats added to the ends of the lid, just as I have done, but did not have hinges; ours does. The understructure is a simple affair built using mortise and tenon; the legs are splayed forward and backward at an angle of 8° to match the box section. I kept the finish simple, just as it was on the original. These pieces were used exclusively in the kitchen and saw a lot of water, so I gave this one the scrubbed look you'll find described on page 25.

BUILDING THE DOUGH BOX

STEP 1. Cut all the pieces to size as laid out in the materials list, then run them through the jointer to clean up the edges.

STEP 2. Build the boards to make the top and bottom of the box unit.

STEP 3. Glue and screw the cleats to the underside of the top.

STEP 4. Sand the top smooth and set it aside.

STEP 5. Go to the lathe and, using the pattern provided, turn the four legs. If you don't have a lathe you can use tapered legs. The procedure is as follows: set your tapering jig to 3° and taper the legs on the two inside edges, making sure you have two right- and two left-hand legs. Begin the taper 4″ down from the top of the leg.

STEP 6. Cut the mortises—1″ deep × ⅜″ × 2″—in the tops of the legs as you see in the drawing.

STEP 7. Set your table-saw miter gauge to 8° off 90 and trim the two end pieces of the apron. Do the same to the ends of the two pieces that will make the end pieces of the box.

STEP 8. Remove the guard from your table saw and set the blade to cut at a depth of 1″.

STEP 9. If you have a tenoning jig, set the back-stop to 8° off the vertical and cut the cheeks. **Note:** Do this first on a piece of scrap stock and test the tenon for fit in one of the mortises.

STEP 10. Mark the shoulders at an angle of 8° (see photo below) to accommodate the angle inside the mortise.

STEP 11. Use your band saw to cut the scrap stock away from the shoulders.

STEP 12. Replace the guard on your table saw and tilt the blade to 8°.

STEP 13. Set your rip fence to 4″, lay the apron pieces flat on the table, outer side up, top edge toward the blade, and trim the edge to 8°; this is so the top of the understructure will fit flush to the underside of the box. **Note:** You can do this step on your jointer if you wish.

STEP 14. Do the same to the tops of all four legs, once again making sure you maintain two left and two right. This is also so the top of the understructure will fit flush to the underside of the box.

STEP 15. Take the four pieces that comprise the apron to the drill press and mill the pocket holes you'll use to attach the understructure to the box unit.

STEP 16. Dry fit all the rails to the legs and lay the lid, upside down, on the structure; all should sit true.

STEP 17. Disassemble all the pieces, sand everything smooth, then glue and reassemble the understructure, clamp it and leave overnight or until the glue has fully cured.

Use a movable square to mark the angles of the tenons to the rails that make up the apron.

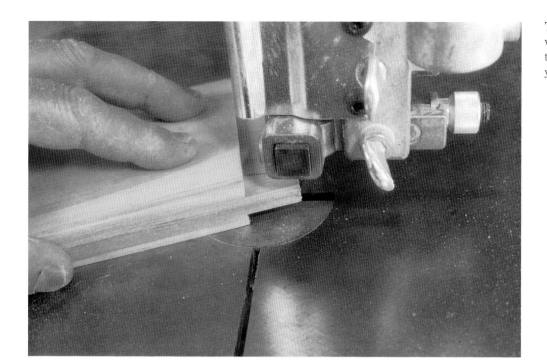

The best way to cut away the waste at the shoulders of the tenons is to do it freehand on your band saw.

Before you mill the mortises, mark the position of each one to ensure you have two left- and two right-hand legs.

STEP 18. With the table-saw blade still set at an angle of 8°, mill the top and bottom edges of the two long sides of the box section so the top and bottom will fit flush.

STEP 19. Take the bottom board to the table saw and mill both edges to an angle of 8° so the bottom and sides will both follow the 8° splay.

STEP 20. Using 1¾″ cut-steel nails and glue, assemble the box unit. **Note:** You'll need to drill pilot holes to accommodate the nails. First use a ⅛″ bit and drill through both pieces of stock, then a slightly larger bit to enlarge

the hole in the outer piece only. Clamp the structure, making sure it's square, and set it aside until the glue is fully cured. **Note:** Bessy makes a clamp that works well when clamping angled boards (see photo page 141).

STEP 21. Place the box unit on the bottom board and mark a pencil line around inside.

STEP 22. Remove the box unit and, using the pencil line as a guide, drill twelve pilot holes in the bottom board—four along each side and two at each end.

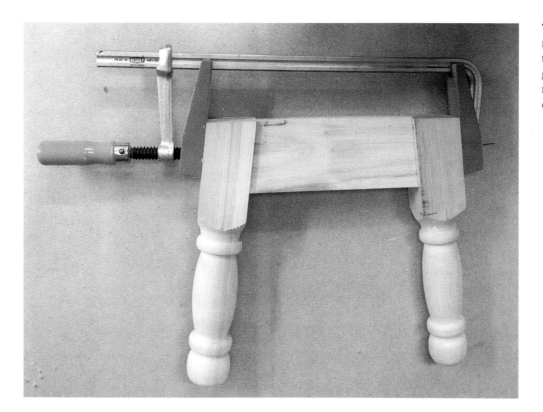

This strange-looking clamp made by Bessy is just the thing for clamping pieces that go together at odd angles. It makes leg assembly on the dough box a snap.

STEP 23. Replace the box unit on the bottom board and using twelve no. 6×2″ screws, fasten the two together. Turn the box unit upside down and place it on the bench.

STEP 24. Place the understructure in place on the underside of the box unit, making sure it's central, and then permanently join the two units together using no. 6×2″ screws through the pocket holes you've already drilled.

STEP 25. Sand all of the faces smooth, but do not attach the lid to the box yet.

STEP 26. Go to the finishing process.

STEP 27. When the finishing is complete, fit the hinges and the lid to the box section.

FINISHING

As previously mentioned, I wanted this piece to look as authentic as possible, so I did little finishing other than some final sanding, some fairly heavy distressing, a light coat of stain to give it the required patina and then the scrubbed pine finish you'll find described on page 25. The finish will darken somewhat with time and wear, but that can only enhance the effect.

Index